THE
Chosen Leah

JOURNEY to the PROMISE

A Kingdom Love Story Of Refinement, Covenant, & Legacy

A SOULWORK BY
Leah VaDol Kirk

Dedication

To the women standing in the hallway between wilderness and promise—
the ones who have cried in secret, warred in silence, and waited with trembling faith—
this is for you.

To the ones who dared to believe again after betrayal,
who kept showing up with hope in one hand and heartbreak in the other—
this is for you.

To every "almost chosen" Leah still wrestling with identity,
to the reflections in the mirror—raw edges, soft bellies, and scars that still speak—
this is for you.

To the woman I used to be,
thank you for surviving.
To the woman I'm still becoming,
keep standing.
And to every daughter who will read these pages and see herself—
may you find strength for your surrender and language for your becoming.

This book is a living altar.
A soul-borne offering carved from obedience, crushed pride, hidden fasts, and reluctant yeses.

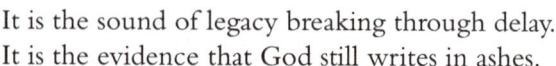

It is the sound of legacy breaking through delay.
It is the evidence that God still writes in ashes.

To my husband, *William Nicolas Kirk*—
thank you for seeing me through Spirit-led eyes and
choosing me on purpose.
You are my Amos 9:13 in motion—evidence that the wait
was worth it.

To my sisters—*Jessica Roberts, Kendie Jackson Bradley, and
Prophetess*—
your covenant love covered me when I forgot how to pray.
You held me up, reminded me of my name, and walked
with me through every chapter.
You are midwives to this message.

To my spiritual home, *Abundant Life Community Worship
Center*—
thank you for being my soil, my sanctuary, and my sending
place.

To *Pastor Daniel Montgomery, Pastor Cheryl Montgomery, Pastor
Jason Morris, and Pastor Carol Morris*—
your obedience made room for my emergence.
You didn't just pour—you *positioned* me.

To the *Father* who authored it all—
thank You for trusting me with this assignment.
For chasing me down, loving me back to life,
and turning my private healing into a public mantle.

This journey was never just about marriage.
It was about identity, refinement, legacy, and discipleship.
It was about becoming the bride long before I met the
groom.
And now, I carry this story not as a survivor—but as a
steward.

Thank you for opening this book.
Thank you for walking with me through the fire and the fulfillment.
Thank you for witnessing the making of a promise—
and the woman entrusted to carry it.

In covenant and calling,
Leah VaDol Kirk

The Divine Path

AUTHOR'S NOTE:
The Blueprint

Before we dive in, it's important you understand this is more than just a love story. It's not just a testimony about heartbreak and hope. It's not even just about kingdom marriage. What you're about to read is a **prophetic blueprint** — revealed by the Holy Spirit, whispered in quiet moments of obedience, and now laid bare for the glory of God.

This book is evidence that when God authors your story, He leaves nothing untouched — not even the math.

What follows isn't just a timeline of events. It's a living, breathing revelation. A sequence of divine breadcrumbs that prove how intricately God designs our journeys — and how faithfully He confirms His word, again and again.

The Structure: 12 Chapters of Prophetic Completion

The book is divided into *12 chapters*, symbolically split between two sections — the *Old Testament* and the *New Testament* — to mirror the arc of my own spiritual journey: from wilderness to promise, from brokenness to covenant.

Biblically, *12* is the number of *divine government, spiritual authority, and prophetic fulfillment*. It shows up everywhere:

- The 12 tribes of Israel
- The 12 disciples of Jesus

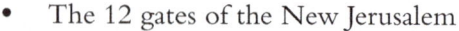

- The 12 gates of the New Jerusalem

For me, the number 12 has personal prophetic weight. Without even realizing it at first, God etched the number across my life like a seal.

The Power of 12

Let's start with my **maiden initials** — *L.V.W.* (Leah VaDol West):

- **L** is the **12th** letter of the alphabet
- **V** is the **22nd**
- **W** is the **23rd**

Break those digits down:
1 + 2 + 2 + 2 + 2 + 3 = 12

Even more mind-blowing? My husband's full name — **William Nicolas Kirk** — also reflects the number 12 when you add up the digits of each letter's position in the alphabet:

- **W** = 23
- **N** = 14
- **K** = 11

2 + 3 + 1 + 4 + 1 + 1 = 12

It's as if God left a *fingerprint* on our union — a quiet seal of symmetry that marked us before we ever knew we were meant for each other.

But here's where the blueprint goes deeper…

There was someone who came before my husband — a man I once believed *was* the promise. I call him **The Refining Forerunner**. We'll unpack his role more in the *Preface*, but for now, what you need to know is this: **even his initials reduced to 12** when calculated the same way.

That's how convincing the counterfeit can be.

The enemy is a master of mimicry — offering *echoes* of divine patterns to distract you from the real thing. The number 12 showed up again, not to confirm my destiny, but to *test my discernment*. It looked like alignment, but it wasn't anointing. It was an echo — not a promise.

THE ACCELERATION OF AMOS 9:13

When my promise truly arrived — when **Will** stepped into the frame — the prophetic shifted. Suddenly, the number **9** began to blaze with Holy Spirit significance.

My **married initials**, *L. V. K.* (Leah VaDol Kirk), carry a new kind of weight:

- **L** = 12th
- **V** = 22nd
- **K** = 11th

Break them down into digits:
1 + 2 + 2 + 2 + 1 + 1 = 9

Nine is the number of *divine finality, birthing, and spiritual fruitfulness*. It signifies the *completion of a cycle* — the moment when labor turns into delivery.

And if that weren't enough? My full married name — **Leah VaDol Kirk** — contains **13 letters**.

Enter the verse that changed everything, the foundation scripture of our union:

Amos 9:13 (MSG): *"Yes indeed, it won't be long now,"* God's Decree. *"Things are going to happen so fast your head will swim…"*

That's exactly what happened. From beginning our courtship in December to our wedding day in May — everything moved with *supernatural speed and precision.* It wasn't rushed. It was *divinely accelerated.* God flipped the script. What felt delayed for years unfolded in *five months flat!*

But here's the part that still seals the deal:

We got married on **May 13th — 5/13**.

We didn't pick the date based on venue availability or family convenience. We didn't even go through a traditional engagement. It was a spontaneous, Spirit-led moment of obedience. After one deep, honest conversation, we skipped the fluff and planned our elopement in *24 hours* — not out of haste, but out of *reverence.*

We simply wanted to honor God by getting into covenant.

And wouldn't you know it?
5 + 1 + 3 = 9

Another divine stamp. Another layer of confirmation. *No accidents. No coincidences. Just God's perfect orchestration.*

This isn't just a story.
It's a *prophetic sign.*

A living, breathing blueprint for every woman waiting on God's timing.

A holy reminder that discernment matters — because not everything that glitters is God.

A testimony that confirms: when God writes your love story, He'll confirm it with *symbols, scripture, and supernatural speed*.

And when it happens?
You'll know.

Preface:
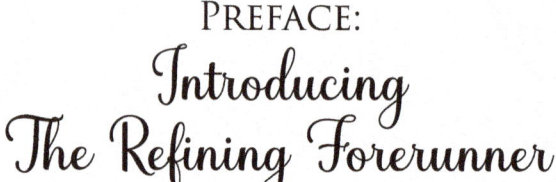
Introducing
The Refining Forerunner

I know some of y'all are already settling into your seats with your spiritual popcorn, ready for some church-girl tea — and in a way… you're not wrong. But before we wander deep into the wilderness of my becoming, I need to introduce you to someone pivotal.

A man I call **The Refining Forerunner**.

I chose this name prayerfully and intentionally. He wasn't my enemy. He wasn't my husband. He wasn't my forever — but he was essential to my becoming.

Much like John the Baptist was sent ahead to prepare the way for Jesus — *"A voice of one calling in the wilderness, 'Prepare the way for the Lord, make straight paths for him'"*[1] — this man arrived before my promise to clear the debris of my doubt and prune the wild, tangled vines of my heart.

He was a mirror, reflecting my deepest longings and insecurities like moonlight dancing on a midnight lake. He was a divine chisel, revealing fractures only the Master Potter could mend.[2] He was the gentle storm that watered my barren

---

1 *Matthew 3:3 (NIV)* — *"A voice of one calling in the wilderness, 'Prepare the way for the Lord, make straight paths for him.'"* See also Isaiah 40:3 and John 1:23.
2 *Jeremiah 18:4 (NIV)* — *"But the pot he was shaping from the clay was marred in his hands; so the potter formed it into another pot, shaping it as seemed best to him."*

fields, the lighthouse flickering in the fog, guiding me toward the shore of God's promise.

He taught me about emotional intimacy, spiritual patience, and the hidden caverns of my heart still waiting to be surrendered. He was the "almost" that sharpened my discernment, preparing me to recognize the "appointed."

He was never meant to be my final destination — merely a signpost on the journey, a divine echo reminding me that the promise is always preceded by preparation. In his imperfections and those fleeting glimpses of goodness, he refined me, forging a deeper dependence on the One who authors every chapter of my story.

And here's where it gets wild — his initials also aligned with the prophetic number 12. We break that down in full in the Blueprint but let me just say this: the enemy doesn't just lie — he mimics. The counterfeit often carries the *form* of the promise without the *anointing*, without the *assignment,* without the *oil.* That numerical echo wasn't confirmation — it was a test. It looked like alignment, but it lacked authority.

In the Blueprint, I shared how the number **12** symbolizes divine authority, and how **9** — the number revealed in both my married initials and our spontaneous wedding date — represents *completion, fruitfulness, and birthing.* That divine alignment wasn't just numerical — it was deeply spiritual. It marked the closing of one chapter and the supernatural beginning of another. That's *Amos 9:13 in motion:* acceleration, fulfillment, and the kind of covenant that can't be explained by logic alone. Only God could orchestrate something so precise.

For his role, I give honor. For his impact, I thank God. He was the one who came before the promise—but was never the promise. The one whose presence revealed my capacity to love deeply, and whose absence taught me to anchor that love in God first. He wasn't the fulfillment—he was the lesson before the legacy.

Journey
to the Promise

June 25th, 2024

*Jeremiah 29:11 — "For I know the plans I have for you,"
declares the Lord, "plans to prosper you and not to harm you,
plans to give you hope and a future."*

Ain't that just beautiful y'all?!
This gotta be the church's favorite scripture!
I done heard it so many times I can quote it in the King
James, NIV, The Message Bible, and the Amplified.
But if I'm really being honest, it's hard to be satisfied…

Now I don't know about y'all, but I've been around a lot of
church folk who are scared of the truth,
Nobody seems to wanna talk about Leah, but they always
wanna talk about Ruth…
And her Boaz,
All the while Leah is known as…
The woman who no man loved, or as some like to call her,
the sister with the lazy eye[3].
Little did they know the journey to her promise would lead
to the Lion of Judah coming through her bloodline[4]!
Home girl is literally the great, great, great, great, great,
great, great grandmother of Jesus — and I love that for her!

---

3 *Genesis 29:17 — "Leah had weak eyes, but Rachel had a lovely figure and was beautiful."*
4 *Genesis 29–30; Matthew 1:1–3 — Tracing Leah's lineage to Judah and ultimately to Jesus.*

But I don't think she knew her journey would lead to her father scheming to marry her off to a dude who stole his brother's birthright by covering himself in fur[5]!
Ain't that 'bout a mess? Talk about a test…

But on a serious note, I think we can all relate to Leah in one way or another.
Her daddy pawned her off, her husband didn't love her, and her sister felt some type of way because she ended up with her man.
These the parts of the story that got you scratching your head at God's ultimate plan.
I mean for real — I'm sure sis was like,
"Why my life gotta be so hard, G?
You just gone keep bombarding me?!
I'm an obedient daughter, a good big sister, and I done had all this man's babies…
When you coming to my rescue? When you gone save me?!

And not only did I have his babies, I gave this ungrateful fool sons…
Reuben, Simeon, Levi…"
But while she was naming the fruit of her womb, she was interjected by the Most High.

"Yes, my daughter, I see your sacrifice and I understand your pain,
Which is why I gave you praise when you birthed your son, Judah…
Through his lineage will come great kings, ruler after ruler!
If you praise me, I will take you from the woman no man loved to the woman loved by all.
The Unlikely Matriarch.
You will be the mother of great patriarchs…
My servant Moses, by way of the Tribe of Levi.

_____

5 *Genesis 27:15–23 — Jacob deceives Isaac by wearing goat skins to imitate Esau.*

And through Judah's lineage, the giant slayer, David the King.
And I won't stop there — I'll bring forth my Son, Savior of the world, the Messiah, King of Kings!

So just trust my plan and focus on me.
Your journey is to a heavenly place,
The victory you will see."

Now I know Leah was shooketh after getting revelation of Jesus!
Moral of the story is the journey to the promise is written by the one who sees us[6].
Even when we feel unseen, unworthy, and unloved,
Our sacrifice of praise brings forth prosperity from our God above.

And I know, I know — it's easier said than done,
But His strength is made perfect in our weakness[7].
The journey to the promise requires the renewing of the mind and testing of faith,
For Heaven's sake! I love that for me!
It is through Him that we endure to the end,
On our journey to victory,
Because of His sacrifice at Calvary.

So just remember to keep your eyes on the Promise Keeper and not just on the promise,
Because I think we can all relate to Leah just a little bit if we're really being honest.

---

6   Genesis 29:31 — "When the Lord saw that Leah was not loved, he enabled her to conceive…"
7   Corinthians 12:9 — "My grace is sufficient for you, for my power is made perfect in weakness."

The Old Testament: The Becoming

CHAPTER 1:

Finding Leah – The Season of Self & Sacred Mess

Before there was a promise, a partner, or even a glimpse of what was coming—there was me. Me and the wilderness. Me, honest and undone, trying to make sense of a season that broke me and built me at the same time. There were no shortcuts, no certainty—just a quiet invitation to keep going, to trust God anyway, and to find strength in the stretch. And before I could step into covenant the way I dreamed it—whole, healed, and fully seen—I had to walk through the unraveling of the one that didn't last.

After leaving my first marriage, I entered what I can only call a season of raw rediscovery — a sacred mess. We didn't divorce right away; it was a long separation, a slow, aching unraveling. I wore my wedding ring like emotional armor, hoping maybe he would fight for me. Maybe he would chase me. Maybe he would show me I was desired. But he didn't. He sat in his pride, never closing the gap I so desperately wanted him to bridge. And so, I wrestled alone, crumbling under the weight of silent prayers and unspoken longings.

Even as I separated, men approached me constantly — as if they could smell the vulnerability, that spiritual perfume clinging to a woman on the edge of something new. But I held my ground, honoring the covenant until I knew I was truly free.

When the divorce was finalized, I stepped into the world free — but fragile. I wanted to become the woman I had always envisioned: confident, radiant, independent. I started my microlocs — a deeply spiritual and physical reclamation of self. My alopecia had always been my secret shame, hidden behind wigs and weaves. But this time, I chose to stand before my mirror and say, "I love you, as you are." I honored my roots, my crown, my softness.

I reconnected with my childhood sweetheart, hoping nostalgia could redeem us. But he spiraled into alcoholism, weaponized my love, drained my resources, and left me questioning every inch of my worth. Then there was the married man who cloaked his deception in sweet words and charm, telling me they lived like strangers and were "almost" divorced. He love-bombed me, but beneath the sugar was a hollow void. Once I saw it clearly, I cut it off before it consumed me.

There was TheRealDeal — short in stature, but once a big presence in my life. He reemerged, pulling me into a smoky haze of cigar lounges and low-lit conversations. But he was unraveling, chasing women, battling a gambling addiction, and drowning in empty thrills. Through him, I discovered a circle of men who became my unexpected teachers. They taught me the games men play, the power of feminine mystery, and how to sit confidently in rooms where I once felt invisible.

Those cigar lounges became my Esther preparation ground[8] — a smoky sanctuary where I learned to listen, discern, and move like a queen. I became the mysterious woman in the red dress, honey-blonde microlocs flowing, always dressed to be seen, always ready for a divine encounter.

I dated all shades and all walks of life — dark-skinned kings with locs, sun-kissed white boys who didn't know how to dress themselves. I explored not to be chosen but to learn what I truly desired. I smoked weed daily, my silent therapist and ritual confidant. I dined alone, relishing the power of a woman who didn't need a companion to feel worthy. I dressed up every time I left the house — not for them, but for me. Because what if I ran into an opportunity, a moment, a divine setup? I was always ready.

There were nights when I sobbed into my pillow, crying out to God, "Where is my husband? Why does it feel like my promise is passing me by?" But there were also nights of deep, soul-soothing peace, where I sipped my drink in a smoky lounge corner, fully content in my own skin.

---

8 *Esther 2:12-17 — Esther's preparation process before meeting the king, a season of purification, adornment, and preparation for destiny.*

I wanted marriage. I wanted covenant. But I also wanted to soak up every drop of my single season — to laugh too loud in cigar lounges, to wear red lipstick and leave imprints on cocktail glasses, to dance alone in my living room like Stella getting her groove back. Only this wasn't about getting it back — it was about discovering it for the first time.

I experimented, I wandered, I healed. Every wrong turn carved me into the woman I needed to become. The wilderness didn't break me. It stripped me, refined me, and prepared me to carry the weight of a real promise. It was the soil where God planted my future legacy.

In this divine mess, I didn't find a husband. I found me.

I found the chosen Leah — refined, radiant, and finally free. The woman who would one day dance freely in front of Egyptian pyramids, head tilted back in confidence, locs whipping through the air, embodying the very freedom she once only prayed for.

This season was messy, beautiful, tragic, and holy — all at once. And I wouldn't change it for anything.

In that wilderness season, I wasn't just waiting. I was becoming. Becoming the woman God had always envisioned, the woman finally ready for the promise beyond the pain.

CHAPTER 2:

The Refining Forerunner – The Almost

---

*J*f Chapter 1 was the wilderness, Chapter 2 was the fire. Not the consuming kind—but the kind that tests motives and reveals what can't last.[9] The next stop in my journey came wrapped in charm and confusion—an "almost" so convincing, I mistook it for destiny. But it wasn't. It was a mirror, not a promise—a lesson I wasn't ready for, but one I couldn't skip. And like most divine disruptions, it didn't look like a warning. It looked like a setup.

We didn't meet on an app, at church, or through a friend. We met at a gas station — *twice*. The first time felt like a moment written straight from heaven: it was raining, I wore a fur vest, feeling unstoppable, on my way to see another man. I pulled up, music playing, energy high. Then he pulled in — dramatic, intentional, as if he was stepping onto a stage meant just for us. He backed into the pump next to mine; eyes locked on me like he had just discovered the missing piece he didn't know he was searching for.

I threw out my handkerchief — an old-school move in a modern world. I made a playful, slightly flirtatious comment about the rain ruining my vest, fully expecting him to catch the invitation. He smiled, stumbled over his words, and we exchanged names right there between the pumps. My heart raced, and I just knew God was scripting something I didn't yet understand.

9 *John 1:23 — John the Baptist declaring himself as "the voice of one crying out in the wilderness, 'Make straight the way of the Lord.'"*

But he fumbled. He didn't ask for my number. I drove off, confused, replaying every detail like a movie reel in my mind: his eyes, my line, that unforgettable pause when he should have asked and didn't. I wondered if I had imagined the spark, but deep down, I believed God was orchestrating something beyond my understanding.

Weeks later, God orchestrated what felt like a divine encore. Same gas station. Same pump. Same magnetic pull. This time, he didn't miss. He asked for my number, and I gave it to him, heart thudding, hope alive. But let's talk about the detail that always left me shook: I lived around the corner from that gas station. It was my neighborhood stop. He, on the other hand, lived 35 minutes away, across a bridge that required a toll just to reach my side of town. What on earth was he doing there that day? The divine choreography was undeniable.

He was everything I had prayed for on my "God, please" list. Not exactly tall, but tall enough to make me feel small when he wrapped those thick arms around me — the kind of arms that fill out every T-shirt just right and make you do a double take every time he walks by. Magnetic, charismatic, spiritually articulate — he carried an anointing that could light up a room and a brokenness that whispered secrets only God knew. He wasn't just a man — he was an experience, the kind that makes you believe every tearful prayer has finally been answered.

But from the very beginning, our connection was always behind closed doors, always at his convenience. I craved dates, long weekends, public affection — all the markers of being cherished. I set my boundaries, reminded myself that I was a woman who wouldn't accept less than I deserved. I knew I was worthy of more, but I didn't know how to get it. I thought if I asserted myself enough, he would rise to meet me. But he never did.

Each time I tried to advocate for my needs, to express my longing for more, I felt him pull away. So, I shrank. I became increasingly accommodating, telling myself that maybe if I bent a little more, he'd finally choose me fully. I twisted myself into shapes God never designed, hoping to become "the one" he'd work for.[10]

The intimacy — emotional and physical — only deepened my soul tie to him. It created a bond so strong that even when I knew he wasn't showing up for me, I couldn't let go. He felt like everything I wanted and what I thought I needed. He was a man of God, and the divine way we met felt like irrefutable evidence that he was my promise.

I can't say with certainty that he loved me in the storybook way I craved, but sometimes love isn't loud — it's in the hidden gestures, the quiet obedience, the moments that slip out when guards are down. He slipped once or twice, saying it playfully, almost like he tossed the word into the air to see if it might land. I never said it back then; I was too busy pretending to protect a heart that was already unraveling thread by thread.

But later — during our fleeting, illusion-wrapped moments at church, when I still believed he was "the one" who just needed space to heal — I finally told him I loved him. It felt acceptable, even Christlike. What would Jesus do? He would love boldly, innocently, without agenda. That was my heart's posture: pure, hopeful, surrendered.

Back then, I brushed off his decision to step away as one of those classic "church excuses" — you know, the ones people use when they don't want to own the real reason: "God told me to." But now, on the other side of heartbreak and healing, I see it clearly. He really was listening to God, even when it hurt him too.

---

10 *Proverbs 4:23 — "Above all else, guard your heart, for everything you do flows from it."*

Funny how sometimes the truest form of love is the willingness to lose you so you can find what's actually meant for you. And for that? I'm thankful — *painfully, beautifully, soul-deep thankful.*

When he invited me to his church, I thought it was the beginning of something real — a true unveiling, an invitation into his world. But what I found was so much deeper than him: I found covenant. I found sisterhood.

That's when I met **Jessica Roberts**, my SISTER, in every sense of the word. She didn't just see me worshiping in the first two rows — she *spiritually* saw me. Led by the Spirit, she approached me after service, asked about my gifts, my story, my scars. Jessica is my *prophetic purpose pusher*. She has this divine finesse: she'll challenge you to greatness, coax your gifts out for the Kingdom, and before you even realize it, you're moving in your calling like it was always second nature. She refuses to let me play small, constantly reminding me that the oil on my life is too potent to be hidden in the shadows. She's a mirror reflecting God's boldest vision for me back to myself, sharper and clearer than I ever dared to imagine.

Through Jessica, I met **Kendie Jackson Bradley**, the big sister I never knew I needed — the worship warrior with a laugh that can heal old wounds and a voice that vibrates straight through your bones. You can always tell when Kendie's not around; the whole room feels a little quieter, a little less electric. To know her is to love her, to be undone by her warmth. She's the one who playfully bullies you in the most loving, big-sister way — equal parts clown, counselor, and cheerleader. Many late nights were spent sitting in my car parked outside her house, me sobbing and unpacking the chaos with the Refining Forerunner. She never rushed me through my heartbreak or belittled my confusion. Instead, she teased me through it, weaving joy into my pain, helping me laugh between the tears while holding up a steady light-house when my spirit was lost at sea.

Together, these covenant connections became my safe harbor, my spiritual lifeboats, my divine hype team — the ones who lifted my arms when I was too tired to fight, prayed me back to life when I was drowning, and reminded me who I was (and whose I was) when I almost forgot. They were the living proof that God will send exactly who and what you need — even when you think you're just following a man to church.

Meanwhile, he began to retreat. We met at Starbucks, and I laid my questions bare: "Why don't I see you outside of church? Why are you pulling away?" His answer cut deep: God told him to give me space. He said he didn't want to, but he had to obey.

I convinced myself this was divine separation — that he needed to heal and would come back whole. I clung to every sweet word he had spoken, every memory, every sign, believing he just needed time.

Then she came. The woman at church. She asked if I was with him because she had been watching us. Women's intuition, sharpened and Spirit-led, never lies. She explained they had a history but weren't seeing each other anymore; she had returned to a man she believed was her "forever." It felt odd that she approached me if it was truly over, but I felt her pain. She told me she had asked him about me but only got fragments. Her words didn't explain everything, but they confirmed what my spirit already knew: *I wasn't crazy.*

I was angry. I was heartbroken. But somehow, I didn't love him less. Instead, I felt an almost holy compassion for his brokenness. It showed me just how deeply wounded he was.

Throughout this wilderness journey, I never truly got over him. Even up to the moment God revealed Will to me — and me to Will — I was still convinced that I had to be patient and wait for the forerunner to return. My sisters Jessica and Kendie kept trying to talk sense into me. They liked to say I was Helen Keller — blind and deaf to the obvious. But they kept pouring into my spirit that the man who was for me would be direct. There would be no confusion, no ambiguity. Just certainty.

To me, that sounded like a fairytale or a theory someone dreamed up on a Pinterest board. I had never actually experienced a man moving with that kind of clarity. But they kept saying it. And somewhere deep inside, my spirit knew it was true. My heart knew it. My mind and my emotions had to catch up later — through the heartbreak.

My sisterhood was everything. Their voices, their support, their example. They held me up when I was stubborn, insistent that this man had to be my husband because "God told me I was in my marriage season." It wasn't until I finally stopped letting my desires scream louder than God's voice that I realized the painful truth: *Yes, God said I was in my marriage season, but He never said this man was my husband.*

That was flesh. That was carnality. That was a soul tie.

He wasn't the promise — he was the forerunner. The almost that almost broke me. The man God used to refine my faith, sharpen my discernment, and teach me the painful price of loving potential over reality.

I learned that emotional connection without covenant is a trap, that vulnerability without true commitment cuts deeper than betrayal, and that being near your calling isn't the same as stepping into it.

God whispered, *"Release what was never yours, so I can reveal what has always been."*

It took spiritual surgery to sever the soul tie. Every unanswered text, every lonely night, every tear-stained prayer was part of God's refining work. I didn't just walk away — I crawled, dragging my brokenness behind me. But even then, I was moving closer to my promise.

CHAPTER 3:

The Father Wound – Trading Performance for Promise

While the world might label my season between "almost" and "appointed" as a waiting room, in reality, it was a surgical suite for my soul. A hidden place where God stripped me down, layer by layer, to heal wounds[11] I didn't even know were dictating my choices — the deepest of which was my father wound.

My relationship with my father is complicated. I love him deeply, and I know he loves me. But love, when mixed with inconsistency, can plant seeds of confusion in a daughter's heart.

My parents divorced when I was just four years old. After the split, my dad moved to Texas while my mom, my two brothers, and I stayed in California. He wasn't gone from my life entirely — but his physical absence left an ache that would echo for decades.

Growing up, I watched my father date different women. It often felt like we, his children, were props in those relationships. Women would buy us gifts, take us on outings, spend money on us — maybe to win his affection, maybe to feel chosen themselves. My dad never truly committed to them, and in that performance, I learned a dangerous lesson: that being loved meant performing.

11 *Psalm 147:3 — "He heals the brokenhearted and binds up their wounds."*

I know my dad did the best he could with what he had. This isn't to villainize him but to highlight the nuanced wound that formed in me. A wound that taught me to search for validation in men who could never truly love or choose me — because deep down, I hadn't yet chosen myself.

But the pain didn't just come from witnessing him cycle through girlfriends. Another deep fracture formed in childhood when I watched him remarry. I was in elementary school — somewhere between third and forth grade — when he wed a woman who already had two daughters. They lived in Texas, while my brothers and I, one of whom is his biological son and one he helped raise from birth — remained in California. And while I tried to embrace these girls as my little sisters, it hurt. Because while he was showing up as a father daily for children who weren't biologically his, we were growing up with only glimpses of him — holiday visits, summer breaks, and sporadic check-ins.

He was parenting in full for another household while we received fragments.

That ache matured into grief when, years later, I saw the same pattern emerge again — but this time with even more tension and emotional exhaustion. In 2019, while I was in a relationship with the man who would become my husband in 2021, we were leaving an event in Dallas, Texas, and driving to New Orleans. My dad was upset that we hadn't made plans to see him while in town. But in my mind, I had flown thousands of miles to be in his state. If he truly wanted to see me, couldn't he have made an effort, too?

In an attempt to avoid tension, we made small talk on the phone. But once again, I found myself being ushered into a phone conversation with a woman I didn't know — someone I hadn't even heard of. He handed her the phone without warning, as if I was supposed to entertain or perform for her comfort. That moment felt all too familiar — a recurring script where I was expected to play the part of the understanding daughter, extending warmth to strangers my father hadn't even taken the time to properly introduce or contextualize.

It wasn't just the awkwardness — it was the lack of transparency. I later found out, through a messy trail of inconsistencies and fragmented stories, that this woman had become his partner. She was young — just a couple years older than me — and their relationship had formed under circumstances that made everything feel even more confusing and painful. And although I won't go into those details out of respect, I will say that the lack of clarity and honesty from my father made me feel used, *again*. Put on display. Pulled into a relationship dynamic that wasn't rooted in trust or truth.

Years later, in 2021, I went to Texas to visit my first nephew for the first time and to spend some intentional time with my best friend, Rachel. She had been by my side through some of the hardest seasons of my life. We met our senior year of high school and remained inseparable for nearly 14 years — the first true experience I had of consistent, sisterly friendship. While there, I ended up seeing my dad in person. We had planned to catch up — just me, him, and Rachel. But he brought his partner along unannounced. And not just her, her young daughter, too.

When they walked into the restaurant, it felt more like a performance than a reunion. She was dressed to be seen — full glam, heels, and a curated presence in a casual bar-and-grill. I was in a sundress and flip-flops, just hoping for a simple, meaningful connection with my father. Instead, I found myself sitting across from a woman I barely knew, feeling like a stranger at my own table.

And what made it worse was the segregation of energy. My dad didn't bridge the gap. There was no effort to draw her or her daughter into the conversation. She sat silently, and he let her. It felt like me and Rachel were having dinner with him, while she was a spectator on the sidelines — one he brought without invitation or explanation.

Eventually, I couldn't stomach the silence anymore. After a trip to the restroom to calm my racing heart, I returned to the table and asked the question I had been holding in: *What is this?* Are you two together? Engaged?

To my surprise, both of them claimed they weren't. She even said, "We're not together right now." Yet I could see the ring on her finger. I could feel the tension in the air — the kind that only comes from unresolved entanglements. My dad, in his usual way, tried to dance around the truth, over-explain, and keep peace. But I was tired of pretending. I told him directly: *You haven't given me an example I can respect. You haven't shown me what to look for in a man. And I can't keep performing like everything's fine when it's not.*

He apologized. But by then, something in me had already shifted.

Two weeks later, they got married. No conversation. No phone call. Just a group message on Facebook Messenger with a Zoom link.

I didn't join.

Not out of spite, but out of hurt. Because after all that confusion, all the unclear dynamics, all the years of feeling like a prop in his parade of relationships — I was once again invited to participate in something I didn't even understand. And now this woman, two years older than me, held the title of "wife."

From that point forward, my relationship with my dad grew even more strained. Holidays, birthdays, random check-ins — I began to disengage. Not because I didn't love him, but because I didn't trust the space. It became harder and harder to feel like I belonged in his world.

Even now, I wrestle with what the future looks like between us. I've released him to the Lord. Released his choices. Released the expectation that he will ever become someone different. But I'm still grieving what never was — and what will likely never be.

That's the honest truth.

But God, in His mercy, has never left me fatherless. He's sent voices — even from afar — to guide me through the fog of identity and brokenness. One of those voices was Pastor R.C. Blakes, a man I discovered on YouTube whose teachings on queen consciousness and womanhood gave me language I didn't know I needed. [12]My current pastors, Daniel Montgomery and Jason Morris, have modeled a kind of fatherly consistency and grace that I deeply cherish. Even my own husband has, in some ways, become a healing balm in that space. It's not perfect. The healing is not complete. But I am in process.

I may never fully untangle the web of emotional and spiritual confusion that formed in me from these years of inconsistency, but I'm learning to stop performing. I'm learning that I don't have to be on display for anyone's comfort. I don't have to say yes when my soul is screaming no. I don't have to wear the mask of a peacemaker at the cost of my own peace.

God isn't transactional. He's relational. And while I once thought I had to earn love — from my father, from men, even from God — I now know that love is my birthright. Not a prize for good behavior, but a gift freely given.

This season was filled with late-night sermons, whispered prayers, worship sets in my room, and honest, soul-deep conversations with God. I had to learn to stop bargaining and start becoming.

I traded performing for promise.

I had to learn that I wasn't overlooked; I was being protected. I wasn't delayed; I was being developed. The father wound taught me that I didn't need to perform to be loved — not by a man and certainly not by God.

---

12 Romans 12:2 — "Do not conform to the pattern of this world, but be transformed by the renewing of your mind."

It took the ache of abandonment, the confusion of romantic missteps, and the wisdom of prophetic voices to finally see myself as God saw me: *chosen, worthy, and loved beyond my wildest imagination.*

Healing didn't come from trying to fix what broke me — it came from releasing it, and remembering I was never forsaken. [13]

13 *Isaiah 62:4* — *"No longer will they call you Deserted, or name your land Desolate. But you will be called Hephzibah, and your land Beulah; for the Lord will take delight in you, and your land will be married."*

Godfidence

June 17th, 2024

Who sent me?
I'm so glad you asked…
I come in the name of Jesus Christ of Nazareth, the Most High God!
See, this isn't a façade. *I'm really like that.*
Better yet, *I'm about that life!*

I know who God says I am and what He says I am.
I'm a Queen — fearfully and wonderfully made. [14]
My confidence comes from the price that He paid!

Many have been called, but I'm one of God's chosen.
I'm a mouthpiece for His Kingdom; I leave no word unspoken.
I'm a daughter of the King — my light shines from within, no kilowatt.
Dim my shine to satisfy your insecurity? *I think not.*

Can't nobody do me better than I can — and that goes for you too!
Look, you gotta remember:
Purpose is not the thing that *you do*…
It's the thing that happens in *others* when you do what you do.

You feel what I'm saying? You see where I'm coming from?
Godfidence comes from valuing your own worth — not

---

14   *Psalm 139:14 (NIV)* — *"I praise you because I am fearfully and wonderfully made; your works are wonderful, I know that full well."*

comparing yourself to others.
It's not about walking into a room thinking you're better than everyone.
It's walking in and not comparing yourself to anyone at all.

Wouldn't it be pointless for the moon to compare itself to the sun,
when it shines in its own time?
See, comparison is the thief of joy,
and no one can make you feel inferior without your consent. [15]

Godfidence comes from an inner witness —
a Holy Ghost boldness from the One who's heaven-sent.
I've got evidence.
I've got *Godfidence.*

I'm a conqueror. I know that I'll win.
I know who I am…
I am victorious — and so are you.

Predestined from the foundation of the earth, [16]
He's given us hope, a future, and an expected end. [17]
God wrote it in His plan…

So, as you go forth in what God has called you to do,
Be who you are. Share your gifts!

Because those who mind don't matter,
and those who matter don't mind.
You are *one of a kind!*

---

15 *Galatians 6:4 (NLT)* — *"Pay careful attention to your own work, for then you will get the satisfaction of a job well done, and you won't need to compare yourself to anyone else."*
16 *Ephesians 1:4 (NIV)* — *"For He chose us in Him before the creation of the world to be holy and blameless in His sight."*
17 *Jeremiah 29:11 (NIV)* — *"For I know the plans I have for you," declares the Lord, "plans to prosper you and not to harm you, plans to give you hope and a future."*

Godfidence radiates from within.
He was bruised for our iniquities, beaten for our
transgressions —
the Ultimate Sacrifice. He died for our sin. [18]
His life positioned you for rebirth.

It would be selfish of you not to pursue purpose
and sow your gifts in this earth.

They say cemeteries are some of the most expensive real
estate,
because that's where good ideas and dreams go to die.
So I urge you, saints —
cultivate the Godfidence within you while you're yet alive,
so when you're called before Him,
you'll hear *"well done"* from the Most High. [19]

---

18 *Isaiah 53:5 (KJV)* — *"But he was wounded for our transgressions, he was bruised for our iniquities…"*
19 *Matthew 25:23 (KJV)* — *"Well done, good and faithful servant… enter thou into the joy of thy lord."*

CHAPTER 4:

The Mother Wound – Learning to Love a Survivor

This one is hard. My mother is a force — a lion-hearted woman, radiant and fierce, a Leo in every sense. But to understand her is to understand that she has always been in survival mode.

Both of my parents were Marines; that's actually how they met, in boot camp. My mother went into boot camp already pregnant with my older brother, Sean, though she didn't know it at the time. The tests didn't detect it, and it wasn't until she was roughly six months along that the truth surfaced. Because of the physical toll, my brother was born prematurely, a tragic entry into the world. He was stillborn and had to be resuscitated. I've always believed he is a walking miracle — you don't survive an entry like that without a divine assignment attached to your name.

My mom is electric — her smile could stop celebrities in their tracks. She is colorful, unapologetic, stubborn, and yet has the softest core that few ever truly see. But I never saw her loved properly. All my childhood memories of her are shaped by her constant fight to pick up the pieces, to provide, to push forward.

After my parents' divorce when I was four, my mom carried the weight of raising us alone. We started going to church when I was around six. There, through influence (some good, some manipulative), she married a man 13 years her senior — an elder in the church. He was the single man who "needed" a wife, and my mom was the single mother of three who "needed" a husband. Church folks called it God's will, but it was pressure, not love.

He was a sanitation worker and a youth Sunday school teacher, yet he drifted from car seats to borrowed couches — a grown man floating through life with no anchor. You'd think a man in his 40s would have found solid ground by then. Not so. I never liked him. In class, he struck my older brother with long sticks meant for discipline but really crafted for humiliation. At home, he made him sleep in the cold tub for wetting the bed, beat him with extension cords, and shattered his spirit piece by jagged piece. My brother carried a rage none of us could decode at the time — a silent storm always brewing beneath his skin. He wasn't the protective big brother I prayed for; instead, he became my sharpest critic, teasing me about my weight, my glasses, my everything — weaponizing his own wounds to dull the ache inside.

At 14 or 15, my brother left to live with my dad in Texas. After that, we grew apart. He became entangled in gang life and incarceration cycles. But today, by God's grace, he's stable, employed, and in a relationship that seems to honor him. I pray he walks into his full miracle one day.

As the only girl, I slipped into the caretaker role for my younger brother, Landon, and did my best to hold everything together. But there was darkness lurking behind closed doors.

I didn't realize at first that my stepfather was grooming me. He'd give me money in secret, let me drive the family cars without a license — gestures I mistook for trust, not manipulation. When I was a teen, he began molesting me. He would come into the room I shared with my younger brother, ensure my brother was asleep, then summon me to the garage to touch me against my will.

One night, I finally snapped. I locked myself in the bathroom and called my mom at her night class. I told her everything. But instead of comfort, I got, "I'll deal with it when I get home." She hung up.

Hours crawled by as I hid in that bathroom, telling my brother I just had a stomachache so he wouldn't worry. When my mom finally came home, she didn't hold me. She didn't ask if I was okay. She didn't look me in the eye and say she believed me.

She simply told me to go to bed — as if sleep could swallow the nightmare whole.

Outside, the yelling cracked through the walls. Words I couldn't fully hear, echoes of a confrontation that felt more like a performance than protection. Deep down, I think she believed me — but belief without action is a quiet betrayal.

I know my mother loves me. But love clouded by unhealed wounds can't always become the safety it's meant to be. She was surviving the only way she knew how — pushing her own pain into the corners, pretending survival was enough to call it healing.

Maybe she thought I'd somehow be "okay" because she decided she was "okay" after her own childhood trauma. But I wasn't okay.

I spiraled. I started acting out — skipping school, sneaking around, chasing any scrap of attention that felt like love. I wasn't carrying on — I was collapsing, piece by piece. That's the thing about generational trauma: *it doesn't ask permission before it roots itself in your story.*

After that, nothing changed. No therapy. No safe space. No justice. The spiral deepened. I kept ditching class, got involved with older boys, lied about my age, and searched for love in reckless places. I even ran away for two days — desperate to scream my truth to anyone who might listen.

Eventually, my mom agreed to let me move to Texas to live with my dad for my senior year. Before I left, we didn't have any deep conversation. She just told me to pack. A week or so later, I was on a Greyhound bus, carrying years of unsaid words and unhealed wounds.

Texas didn't heal me; it simply gave my brokenness a new stage. My dad worked nights, leaving the house as empty as the space inside my heart. I was 16, seeking solace in the arms of older boys, men in their twenties who mistook my trauma for maturity. I played grown before I ever learned what girlhood truly meant.

There was no counseling, no safe place to lay my story bare — not because my family didn't care, but because they didn't know how. They were carrying their own silent wounds, unspoken scars inherited and passed down like heirlooms. My pain wasn't intentionally ignored; it was simply left unheld, unaddressed, unseen.

So, I became a master of tucking it away, performing "okay," hoping someone might look close enough to see the ache behind my bright eyes. But no one did — and I didn't know how to ask them to.

Years later, my mom finally divorced her husband — six years after I told her about the abuse. That broke something deep inside me. *How could she stay?* But now I understand trauma is a prison with invisible bars. She wasn't strong enough to leave then.

When I finally confronted her as an adult, she acted like she didn't remember. She offered to help me press charges, but it felt hollow — like words echoing in an empty room. I truly believe she blocked it out to protect herself, to keep her own fragile world from crumbling.

To this day, my truth has never been fully acknowledged. I used to want to scream his name from the pulpit — "Frostee Lynn Rucker!" — to tear down the silence that nearly swallowed me whole. I grew up in a culture that preached, "What happens in this house stays in this house." But that silence almost destroyed me.

I'm not here to blame. I'm here to tell the truth. To reclaim my voice. To remind myself that the fault was never mine. That healing doesn't mean pretending it didn't happen, but standing in the light and saying, *"It did — and I survived."*

My younger brother eventually grew strong and protective, his body becoming a fortress even our stepdad couldn't tear down. His rage, though often misdirected, was his armor — a shield he crafted from shards of our shared pain. Today, our relationship is distant. But my love for him remains, unwavering and quiet, like a lantern in the dark.

He has two sons of his own now. I've only met the eldest — a brief, passing connection that feels more like a flicker than a flame. The truth is, our childhood wounds didn't just break us; they scattered us like seeds on dry, cracked earth.

We grew up strangers to our own lineage. Uncles, aunts, cousins, grandparents — they were more ghost stories than real people. Those blurry memories are why I hold my chosen family so tightly today. It's not that I wouldn't claim my blood; it's just that planting seeds in hardened, unfamiliar soil at this stage feels almost futile.

I keep sparse connections with two cousins — one from my mom's side, one from my dad's — but that's where the branches stop. My dad's parents are both gone now. His father passed just yesterday as I write this, and his mother two years before. I don't know what to say to him because I never really knew them. Our relationship is already strained, and while I know he's hurting, I ask myself: is it truly my responsibility to bridge gaps that were never built for me?

My mom's side is its own maze. Her relationship with her mother is more of a tolerated obligation than a bond. She calls her by her first name when she's frustrated, and "Mom" only when she must — an unspoken code that reveals generations of pain. Her father passed years ago, and I'm not sure she ever really grieved. Sometimes, I wonder if she would even cry if her mother passed, or if her armor would simply tighten around her heart.

Maybe I'm reaching. Or maybe this is the inherited ache of a daughter trying to decipher pain that was never hers to carry but somehow became her inheritance.

My mom and I are still figuring each other out. After I left Texas, we've mostly been physically distant, except for a few years she lived in Washington before moving to Florida. Our relationship has always felt more surface than soul-deep. We bond over fashion, travel, beauty, and our love for our dog babies — the light-hearted things that keep us orbiting each other.

I love her. I honor her. She's my one and only mother, and that will always live in a protected place within me. But being close to her in proximity is heavy. She's vibrant, fierce, unstoppable — and sometimes, she's simply too much to hold all at once. I've learned to take her in gentle doses, not out of disrespect, but as an act of self-preservation.

We don't talk every day. Sometimes, months pass before we hear each other's voices on a call. We update each other via text, sharing glimpses of our lives until we finally FaceTime and unravel it all in long, meandering conversations. She tells me about her dating life, and I share my projects and my marriage.

She is my loudest cheerleader on social media, always hyping me up, leaving comments, telling everyone how proud she is of me. And I know she truly is. I love that about her — her unwavering ability to root for me from afar.

Our connection might not mirror those deeply entwined mother-daughter bonds I sometimes envy, but I'm grateful for the bond we do have. No, she isn't my "bestie," and we don't live close enough for spontaneous brunches or shopping trips. But I'm happy to see her thriving and glowing in Florida, living her best life in her own way. I want nothing but joy for her, and I know she wants the same for me.

I'll keep working on our relationship — step by step, memory by memory — praying we can continue to create moments rooted in healing rather than haunted by old wounds.

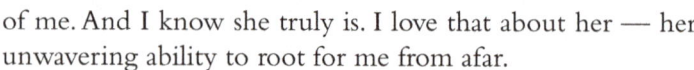

Author's Note:
A Final Word to Frostee

*I don't know if you will ever read these words, Frostee
(yes, spelled F-R-O-S-T-E-E), but I want you to know that I forgive you.*

*I understand the spirit realm — I know that the enemy can use anyone
who allows themselves to be a vessel. And for reasons I will never fully
understand, you chose to open that door.*

*This truth does not excuse what you did. It does not minimize my pain.
But it does free me from carrying the weight of your choices on my back
any longer.*

*I speak this truth to honor my own heart, to reclaim my voice, and to
stand in the light of my healing. By consequence, it exposes you — but it
also exposes me to a deeper level of freedom I didn't know I still needed.*

*I pray you have truly repented. I pray you never violated another young
person's innocence again. I pray that before you leave this earth, you find
real peace with God, because eternity is real, and hell is hot.*

I choose forgiveness — not for you, but for me.

CHAPTER 5:

The Covenant Community – My Chosen Family

They say you can't choose your family, but God showed me otherwise.

After years of wilderness seasons — loving the wrong men, silencing my voice, losing pieces of myself — I finally found a sanctuary for my heart: Abundant Life Community Worship Center in University Place, Washington.

But to truly understand the miracle of Abundant Life, you have to know where I came from.

My first church in Washington? Let's just say it was giving Mean Girls but in church hats. If you weren't born into one of the established families, you always felt like an outsider. At first, I was embraced, but then slowly phased out — the silent competition, side-eyes, and those "God bless her" fake smiles left me feeling unseen and deeply lonely.

Then came the second church. Whew, chile. What is it with me and church guys? I knew I wanted a man of God, but my goodness. Do I know how to pick them. You'd think my obsession with "God-fearing men" would have protected me, but apparently, my type was "dudes who can quote Corinthians but can't commit."

I thought I was starring in a holy love story — plot twist: I was just another extra in his personal church harem. This man had a whole collection, and apparently, I was just the latest shiny addition to the roster. The betrayal? Public. The humiliation? An Oscar-worthy meltdown moment. And the grand finale? He left me for his mistress... who also just so happened to be my friend. Because of course. Insert the biggest, most dramatic eye roll in human history. You truly can't make this stuff up — even Netflix would cancel this script for being too messy.

The leadership never addressed my pain. When my marriage to my former spouse ended, that shame just piled on. I felt ostracized, deeply judged, and completely alone. I left that church and didn't return anywhere for about two and a half years. I told myself I was fine, that I could heal solo — but my soul was starving for true community and spiritual covering.

Then, the one who played that refining role in my journey finally invited me to Abundant Life. It took him a while—hesitant, perhaps, but spirit-led nonetheless—and for that, I'm forever grateful. That invitation cracked open the door to my real healing.

The moment I walked in, I was embraced. Loved on. Welcomed into a space that felt safe, authentic, and deeply genuine. There was no competition, no cattiness — just pure, kingdom love.

Abundant Life Community Worship Center calls itself *"a place to call home,"* and it truly is. From day one, my pastors — Pastor Daniel Montgomery and Pastor Cheryl Montgomery — along with Assistant Pastors Jason (Pastor J) and Carol Morris, wrapped me in spiritual safety and guidance. They poured into me, prayed over me, and celebrated every gift I dared to reveal.

Pastor Dan, lovingly nicknamed "Santa Claus" by his wife Cheryl, is the most giving pastor I've ever seen or experienced in my upbringing. He believes that ministry should be free and accessible to everyone. Any time the church hosts an event, his priority is ensuring it doesn't cost the people anything. He says the kingdom should be funded from inside the house so that anyone who walks through our doors in need can do so without shame or financial burden. That kind of generosity isn't just theory for him — he lives it. He makes it a point to learn names, greet new visitors, and go out of his way to personally welcome everyone. That's how I began feeling so loved at Abundant Life: *because my pastor sought me out.* I didn't have to chase leadership down or feel intimidated approaching him — he came to me. And in just our second conversation, while I was only sharing fragments of my story, he discerned that I would write a book one day. He said it plainly, and it was prophetic. That moment has never left me.

His wife, Pastor Cheryl, is equally powerful in her own right. She is witty, sharp, and straightforward in the most grace-filled way. You can tell just by being around her that she is deeply intuitive and discerning. She's also hilarious — her sarcasm is unmatched — and I personally love the way she delivers truth. There's no guessing with her. She doesn't dress up her words with fluff or perform prim-and-proper "first lady" theatrics. She's real, and she's rooted. Her rebuke comes wrapped in love, but you'll still feel the weight of it — and that's why I trust her.

Pastor J and Pastor Carol stand for marriage like no one else. When Will and I decided to skip the engagement and elope, putting it all together in less than 24 hours, they didn't even blink. Pastor J wrote us custom vows and created a gorgeous, personalized marriage certificate. Pastor Carol brought a ceremonial broom for us to jump — a beautiful touch that blended tradition and spirit. They didn't just officiate; they championed us with joy.

Pastor J is also the one who baptized Will — a moment so defining it instantly bonded them. He checks on Will regularly, and Will treasures that space. As a man who has struggled to find safe brotherhood, Will is so grateful.

Pastor Carol is an absolute powerhouse on stage. When she gets up there, you already know: Heaven is about to drop a remix! But off stage? She's silly, playful, and warm — teasing Pastor J, loving on the children, and moving with this quiet grace that just wraps you up. We share a kindred spirit — both creatives, both event visionaries, both fierce about nurturing other women. Watching her lead our wives' group alongside Pastor Cheryl is a masterclass in love and dedication.

Jessica — my prophetic sister, my purpose pusher, my iron sharpener [20]. She doesn't just see potential; she demands it show up and serve the kingdom, no excuses. She's done this for me time and time again, and she's done the same for Will, encouraging him to explore gifts he didn't even know he had.

Even though she's younger than Will by a couple of years, she carries the wisdom and boldness of a seasoned general — which is exactly why Kendie and I love to tease her, calling her Joe Jackson and Ike Turner. She's tiny (literally half my size!), but her personality is larger than life. Tiny but mighty — that's her all day. She's family. We wouldn't change a single thing.

Will's background is in graphic design. He spent years in the secular space, creating magic for big-name artists and moving in circles most people only dream about. But when God started transforming his heart, he felt a holy pivot — he didn't want to build clout for the world anymore; he wanted to create for the Kingdom.

Enter Jessica: the ultimate kingdom catalyst, spiritual hype woman, and professional "pull-the-gift-out-of-you-even-when-you-hide-it" coach.

At the Juneteenth 2025 celebration at Stewart Heights Park in Tacoma — yes, that one with over 20,000 people in attendance — we pulled up to support Jessica and her sisters' anointed group, *R3FRESH*. And listen… let me slide in this quick flex: that same day, your girl (hi, me!) was featured on Fox13 Seattle News. I literally got stopped mid-strut by an interviewer who said I looked exactly like the radiant energy they needed for their segment. God said, *"Arise and shine,"* and I took that personally.

---

20 *Proverbs 27:17 — "As iron sharpens iron, so one person sharpens another."*

Meanwhile, Will — in true "I'm-just-chillin" fashion — grabbed his gimbal and iPhone 11 Pro and started capturing moments like he was on assignment for Vogue meets Heaven's highlight reel. He wasn't trying to make a name for himself; he was just vibing, doing what felt natural.

Jessica saw the finished recap video and instantly called out the gold. Like the purpose activator she is, she didn't just see a fun hobby — she saw a hidden gift waiting to break through. She started pushing him, watering that seed, encouraging him to lean all the way in and use it for God's glory.

Will doesn't do it for the money. He does it because he genuinely wants to help his sister Jess and support anything she's building. He recently told me, "I'm good with doing this ground floor work. I just want to help her, and I appreciate that she's giving me access to opportunities I wouldn't have otherwise." He's all in, no ego, just pure service and gratitude — and watching that unfold makes my heart so full.

Jessica's husband, Jeff, is another rock. He checks on Will consistently, and they've built a rare, authentic brotherhood. Will often says how hard it is for men to find safe spaces for vulnerability, but Jeff creates that. Their hangouts are therapy, and I'm so thankful. Jeff and I have our own playful banter too but seeing how he pours into my husband means everything to me.

Kendie — my warrior sister — and her husband, Demetric, have become unexpected anchors in our community tapestry. In the beginning, Demetric operated almost entirely behind the scenes, sending silly videos on Facebook and Instagram, making us laugh from the shadows. He's super introverted and usually keeps to himself, content in his own quiet lane.

But every time Kendie would come home, bubbling over with stories about our gatherings and the laughter and breakthroughs we shared, it slowly opened his heart to us. Even when he wasn't physically present, he embraced us as his sister and brother, simply because his wife loves us so deeply — and that, to me, is so beautiful. I adore that tender, loyal part of his heart.

Slowly but surely, he started stepping out of the background, showing up to couple hangs and park gatherings, letting his warmth and wit shine. And let me tell you — that man can throw down. Chef, baker, flavor alchemist — he's all of the above. Anytime we plan a gathering, we practically tackle Kendie to make sure she brings something from *Dee's Kitchen*. Every cake is impossibly moist, every dish crafted to savory perfection. Homie really needs to start a food truck or a restaurant (and yes, we're working on that dream).

Watching his bond with Will deepen feels like watching God stitch hearts together in real time, one shared plate and inside joke at a time.

Then there's Caroline — my "Sweets." *Why Sweets?* Because every time I hear her name, Sweet Caroline starts playing in my head like a random TikTok sound I can't escape (ba-ba-ba!). It's basically her personal theme song, and now you'll never un-hear it either.

She's service personified: a wife, a mom of two, and somehow still everyone's personal MVP. She shows up, pours out, and makes you feel like you've just been wrapped in the coziest blanket straight from God's throne room. Her husband Ort and their two children aren't just part of her village — they're part of mine. Together, they've become like a second family to my fur babies, Biggie and Jenasys. Ort has become a true brother to me, and their kids are like my niece and nephew. Their entire household makes my heart feel covered.

We first met through our WOW Life Group — she's Jessica's stepsister — and over time, our bond grew naturally and beautifully. As our friendship deepened, I began to open up about my story. Even before I shared it all, Sweets had already sensed the truth in her gentle, intuitive way. She might not consider herself prophetic just yet, but God has clearly given her a gift of discernment that's blooming in real time.

She noticed Will watching me from the beginning — his eyes quietly tracking me like a faithful bodyguard at church. But instead of blurting it out or pushing her thoughts on me, she just planted soft, spirit-guided seeds. Quiet observations, knowing smiles, and those little "hmm" moments that only a true sister can give.

Caroline supports all my creative dreams, ministry efforts, and life pivots. We walk together, and she lovingly watches my fur babies when I travel. She treats them like her own, calling them her niece and nephew — a detail that gives me so much peace when I have to be away.

Abundant Life isn't just a church. It's my chosen village[21]. My refuge after years of storms. My safe harbor after church hurt and spiritual homelessness. Here, I don't have to perform or pretend. I'm celebrated simply for being Leah — healed, healing, radiant, chosen[22].

God doesn't just give us promises; He gives us people to help carry them[23]. My community at Abundant Life is living proof.

For every embrace, every belly laugh, every tear-soaked prayer at the altar — I'm forever thankful.

---

21 *Psalm 68:6 — "God sets the lonely in families, he leads out the prisoners with singing; but the rebellious live in a sun-scorched land."*
22 *Peter 2:9 — "But you are a chosen people, a royal priesthood, a holy nation, God's special possession, that you may declare the praises of him who called you out of darkness into his wonderful light."*
23 *Ecclesiastes 4:9–10 "Two are better than one, because they have a good return for their labor: If either of them falls down, one can help the other up. But pity anyone who falls and has no one to help them up."*

CHAPTER 6:

Becoming Her Before Him – The Sacred Season of Healing & Becoming

There's a divine stillness between heartbreak and promise—a quiet place where heaven doesn't speak, but watches. Where God lets you wrestle with the weight of what you thought you knew, until your spirit catches up to the truth He already planted.

This season wasn't just about waiting for a husband. It was about learning to become the *bride of Christ* first, before I could ever become a bride to a man. It was about allowing God to heal the parts of me that still craved external validation, that still searched for love in broken places, that still held onto unworthy attachments like security blankets.

I served in ministry at Abundant Life — singing on the worship team, co-leading the Women of Worth life group, coordinating events, pouring my heart into every detail. My gifts had been prophesied over me so many times, yet they had laid dormant, waiting for my full "yes." In this season, I gave God my whole yes — no disclaimers, no bargaining, no timelines.

Nights were hard. The bed felt cold, the house echoing with silence. I would lie awake wrestling with desire — for love, for companionship, for intimacy. I missed the safety and permission of marital sex. The Word says it plainly: *"It is better to marry than to burn with passion"* [24] — and oh, I was burning.

But I also knew this fire wasn't meant to consume me; it was meant to refine me.

I stopped smoking weed. I stepped away from the cigar lounge and the false intimacy of male attention. Friendships with men that weren't serving my destiny fell away naturally, like dead leaves in autumn. I chose consecration — not because it was easy, but because my spirit craved purity more than my flesh craved comfort.

When the Refining Forerunner finally withdrew, what began as his choice became mine. Abstinence transformed from a forced season to a holy offering. I began fasting, praying in tongues for hours, receiving divine downloads, and letting God wash away every residue of soul ties.

My sisters in Christ would always tell me how much I inspired them: my confidence, my style, my consistent presentation of beauty and grace even in the waiting. They didn't see the nights I cried myself to sleep, or the mornings I had to hype myself up just to get out of bed. But I showed up — for them, for me, for God.

It was in this season that my leadership began to sharpen. I poured into other women, encouraging them to reclaim their radiance, their power, their worth. Even without biological children, I began to feel the weight of my spiritual motherhood. It was prophesied many times that I would be a spiritual mother to many — a notion that felt wild for a woman with no children. But my heart always knew: I was built to nurture, to protect, to empower.

---

24 *Corinthians 7:9* — *"But if they cannot exercise self-control, they should marry. For it is better to marry than to burn with passion."*

I began to understand that becoming a wife wasn't about preparing for a wedding — it was about preparing to steward God's love on earth.

Yes, there were moments of fear. I was 31, no children, no prospects, haunted by thoughts of "geriatric pregnancy" and time slipping away. I saw happy families, felt the sting of comparison, wrestled with envy. But God kept reminding me: *"Your story is different on purpose."*

And in the midst of all this, God confirmed something monumental: *that I would write a book about my kingdom marriage journey.* This revelation came right in the thick of it—shortly after that infamous Starbucks conversation, when he told me he needed to give me space because "God told him to."

That very day, God ministered to my heart and told me I would one day share my journey publicly. And like always, I ran with it too quickly. I started writing as if *he* was my husband—joke's on me! I stalled out like a car with a bad starter. It was as if God snatched the pen back and said, *"Not yet, daughter."*

I didn't realize I was jumping ahead because I didn't yet have the revelation that he wasn't my promise. I had to walk out a whole series of divine lessons first. But now, here I am — writing this book in real time, exactly as God intended.

I remember May 30, 2024 — the final session of our Women of Worth life group season one. Jessica invited a prophetic speaker named Kristal. We'd never met; she knew nothing about me. During worship, she moved around the room quietly, and I tried to avoid her gaze. But she locked eyes with me and read me for filth — in the most holy, necessary way.

She prophesied over me, calling forth gifts I had buried, mentioning my poetry journal and my love for curating beautiful, spirit-filled gatherings. She affirmed God's spotlight on me in that season and urged me to keep saying yes without fear. I still have the audio recording as proof — *every single word has come to pass.*

People who don't understand might think this is "spooky," but I know God's voice. I know His language. My community knows it too. God used these moments to show the world that I wasn't crazy when I said I was in my marriage season — and He confirmed it quickly.

I remember November 3, 2024 — standing in front of my whole church, testifying about my single season and sharing my spoken word piece titled *Look at God: A Test of Faith.* From that moment on, everything changed.

God had me share my heartbreak, my hope, my healing — all on public display. He told me my marriage would be an example for many, my story an encouragement for those who thought God had forgotten them.

I knew I had become her, because God trusted me to carry this testimony. I was finally ready to carry my marriage mantle — but only after first carrying my individual mantles.

This was my season of healing and holy refinement — the waiting breath of God just before destiny came knocking on the door.

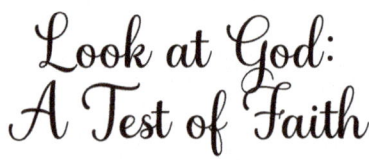

Look at God: A Test of Faith

November 3rd, 2024

Mmmhmmm! I see you!
Looking at me, looking at her, looking at him, looking at them, looking at this, looking at that...
Uhh uhh...don't do that!
You're focused on the wrong things.
What you really need to do is, look at God.
Hold up, I'm not sure you heard me, I said *LOOK AT GOD!*
Look at God and look to God.

Remember Him?
Alpha and Omega, King of Kings, Lord of Lords, Creator of Heaven and Earth, Ancient of Days...
Omnipotent in all His ways.
Divine Creator with a plan so perfect and true.
He has a greater purpose for all that you've been through.

Now I'm not negating the pain, the struggle, and the stress.
A hurt so bad like your heart would fall from your chest.
That real disappointment...
All the delays and denials.
Standing on His promises but still going through trial after trial.

Battling with doubt, abandonment, and fear.
Wondering if God sees you, does He even hear?
Is He there? Does He care? Or is He just sitting back

watching me in torment?

21 questions and not one of them answered, but you've already given your consent.

You gave your YES, in obedience, and then you said yes again.

Time after time, hoping that at some point you'd win.

Standing firm on His promises, even when the ground got shaky.

Meditating scripture, He said He'll never forsake thee. [25]

Circumstances not lining up with His word...

Can I trust my instincts and intuition? Questioning what you heard...

Now I'm not gone hold you. Your feelings are 100% valid. BIG FACTS!

But there's a difference between facts and truth.

Now imma need you to put your intellectual caps on, 'cause I'm finna take you to school.

Truth is a higher standard by which facts are judged.

Fact is a piece of information, a reality that exists, observed by your experience.

As we know, experiences can change. FACT.

They are not universal or permanent.

So as a believer, although your current experience may be painful...

What is constant, what is true...

Jesus is The Way, The Truth, and The Life, and His plan is to prosper you and not to harm you. To give you life, and life more abundantly. [26]

THAT is the truth!

---

25 *Hebrews 13:5 — "I will never leave you nor forsake you."*
26 *John 10:10; Jeremiah 29:11 — Jesus promises life more abundantly; God's plan to prosper, not harm.*

Unchanging, unwavering, and ever constant.
The foundation of our belief system. Our faith is God sent.

Now I'm not claiming any of this is easy. This isn't milk for
infants, it's meat for the mature.
Longsuffering is a Fruit of the Spirit; we are called to
endure. [27]
Trials and tribulation are a part of the process.
Jesus is our Biblical example of what the spiritual law says.

His earthly journey showed us that between the anointing
and the appointing,
there will be disappointing.
"Father, if it be Your will, take this cup from me."
But even He submitted His will through His sacrifice at
Calvary. [28]

My point is, there is purpose for everything that you're
going through.
It's all part of a divine plan...
Orchestrated by our Creator, The Holy Son of Man.
An invisible God with visible wonders.
He can cause the sun to shine or call down rain and
thunder.

With Him, all things are possible.
Strength renewed and joy unspeakable.
I know right now that seems farfetched and sometimes
unbelievable.

This walk with Him is a choice and the testing of our faith
is sure.
It's meant to strengthen our covenant and make our
relationship secure.

---

27 *Galatians 5:22 — Longsuffering as a Fruit of the Spirit.*
28 *Luke 22:42 — "Father, if you are willing, take this cup from me; yet not my will, but
yours be done."*

Draw nigh unto Him and He will give you rest. [29]
Providing relief and comfort in the midst of your test.

Now I know this word isn't very satisfying to the ear,
But as mature believers, we must discern and heed what we hear.
Because sometimes, the only way out is through.
And when you're through, the destination will be there,
but the journey is about becoming YOU!

Becoming the best version of yourself, fully submitted and reliant on The Savior.
Focused on purpose and not people, disciplining yourself in Christ-like behavior.

You see this walk with Him is not about the tangible things
He promises to give you if you're faithful.
It's about detaching from things of the world, renewing your mind, being made over.
Allowing Him to complete His perfect work in you, detoxing you sober.

All this to say, there's no simple answer for the when, the why, and the how.
Focus on your heart posture, and on what God is doing now.

Yes, it's painful, but you're not numb.
Yes, it gets lonely, but you're not alone.
Yes, you're confused, but you haven't lost your mind.
Yes, you're wounded, but not defeated.
Yes, you're tempted, but you haven't given in...
LOOK AT GOD! God is keeping you in this season, in the midst of it all.
So, hold your head high, press forward, and stand tall...
Because after all, it's just a test of faith.

---

29 *Matthew 11:28 — "Come to me, all you who are weary and burdened, and I will give you rest."*

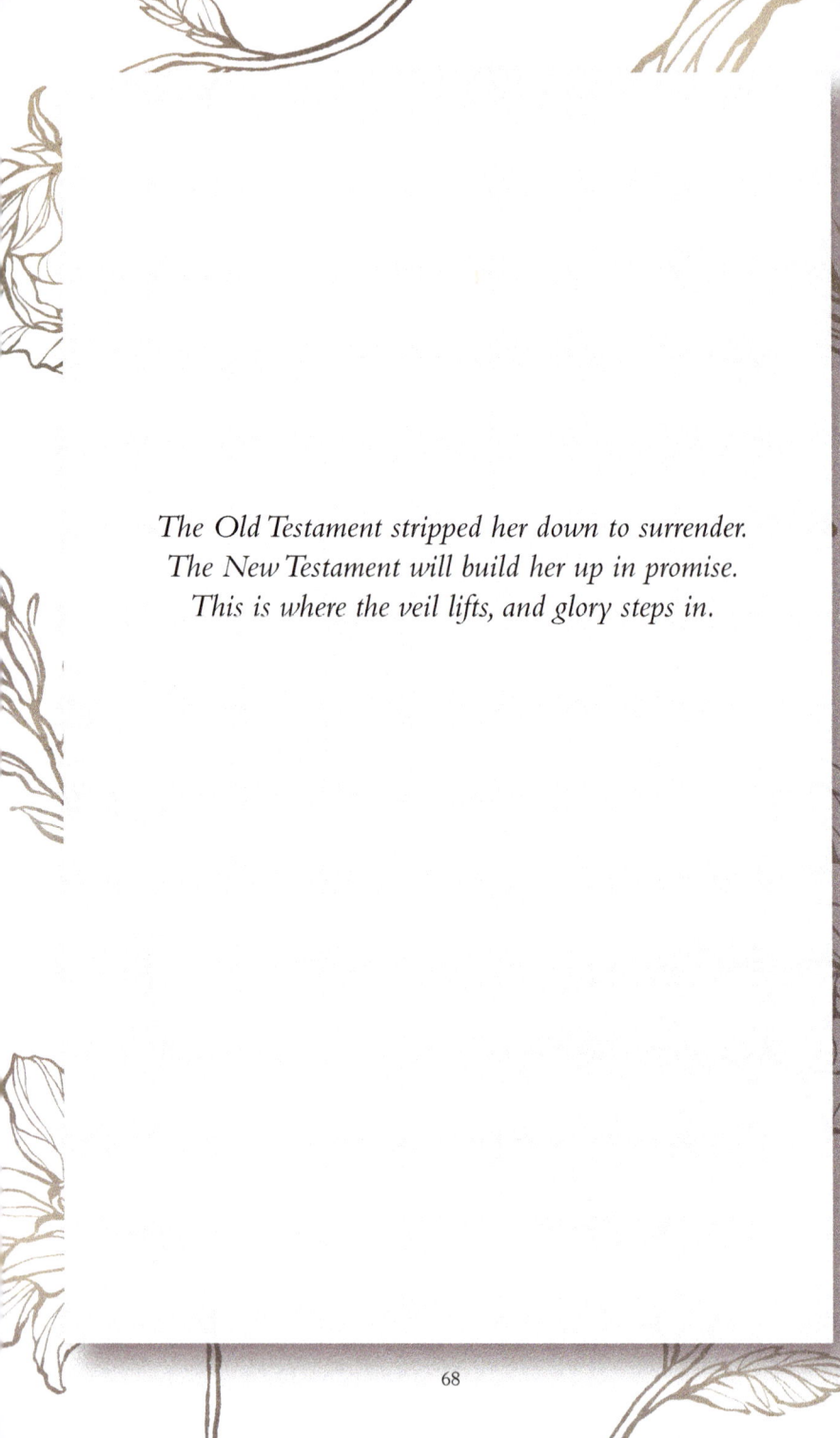

The Old Testament stripped her down to surrender.
The New Testament will build her up in promise.
This is where the veil lifts, and glory steps in.

The New Testament: The Fulfillment

CHAPTER 7:

The Promise in Plain Sight – Enter Will

*I*f the Refining Forerunner was the test, then Will was the confirmation — not loud or flashy, but steady, planted, and spoken by God long before I had ears to hear it. But even before the promise began to stir, before there was a spark or a sign, there was a man walking faithfully — quietly, humbly — on his own road to redemption.

Will's story begins at a sports store in the Tacoma Mall. He wasn't there looking for anything profound — just running errands like any other day. But God doesn't need grandeur to orchestrate destiny. One of the brothers from Abundant Life worked there, and what began as casual small talk transformed into a divine invitation. The topic shifted to God, then to church. Will mentioned he didn't have a church home, and the brother extended the invite without fanfare. Just an open door.

At the time, Will lived five minutes away from Abundant Life. He often drove by the building, not knowing that one day, he'd walk through those doors and never look back. It wasn't random. It was precise — divine GPS at its finest. What Will didn't know then, and what I couldn't see yet, was that his steps were already aligned with mine.[30]

---

30 *Jeremiah 29:11 — "For I know the plans I have for you, declares the Lord…"*

Will is an only child — no siblings, no church upbringing, no spiritual family in the traditional sense. His father, a Black man, was estranged from him for reasons layered and unresolved. His mother, of German descent, had no family in the States. In the natural, Will was alone. But spiritually, God was cultivating something deep in him — a slow, quiet sanctification.

By the time Will walked into Abundant Life in August 2024, God had already been pruning and drawing him. He was detoxing from his past life — the music, the partying, the environments that no longer served his soul. He had lost his passion for secular graphic design work and was in a season of soul-deep refinement. He told me later that after his last heartbreak — one that ended in betrayal and left him hollow — he truly believed he'd never marry. He imagined a future of flings, solitude, and maybe contentment, but not covenant.

And yet, during that time, he chose celibacy. Two years. Not just as an act of consecration, but perhaps also as a protective layer — shielding himself while God did the internal work. He wasn't hiding. He was healing. And that level of self-control — that level of intentionality — was so rare and admirable, even before I knew the full story.

He started attending Abundant Life faithfully, eventually choosing to be baptized. I watched that baptism from across the sanctuary, unaware of what God was preparing. One of the brothers later told him that in the video footage of his baptism, there was a strange glitch — the screen was cloudy when Will went under the water, but as soon as he came up, the video became crystal clear. No one could explain it technically. But spiritually? We both know it was symbolic. *A washing away. A rebirth. The old man buried. The new man risen.*[31]

---

31 *2 Corinthians 5:17* — *"Therefore, if anyone is in Christ, the new creation has come: The old has gone, the new is here!"*

Will showed up with his physical Bible every week — and my pastor, Daniel Montgomery, made it a point to celebrate him for that from the pulpit. In a world of Bible apps and distractions, that small choice stood out.[32] He sat in the first two rows, on the opposite side of the sanctuary from where I usually sit. Always clean-cut, well-dressed, and deeply engaged in worship. Hands lifted. Eyes closed. No performance. Just presence.

And yet — I barely noticed him.

It wasn't that he wasn't there. It's just that my heart was still tethered to the Refining Forerunner. I was spiritually veiled, emotionally unavailable, convinced I was still in the waiting room for "the one" to return. Meanwhile, Will was already in the building.

And even though I hadn't noticed him, others had noticed him noticing me. It wasn't dramatic or obvious—just quiet moments of attention. They saw how he watched me worship. How he paid attention to my joy when I laughed with my sister circle in the foyer. How his eyes followed me

32 Luke 14:10 — "But when you are invited, take the lowest place… then you will be honored in the presence of all the other guests."

through the sanctuary—not out of lust, but with something softer. Steadier.

He never made a move. Never lingered too long. He was intentional about not being "that guy"—the one who comes to church to find a woman instead of seeking God. Will came for the Word. And yet, without even trying… he saw me.

At first, Will was shy. The "Welcome Song" — a cheerful moment where we walk around and greet new faces — became his confidence training ground. He told me that when he first started attending, those few minutes felt like spiritual exposure therapy. He had to push himself to walk up to strangers, shake hands, and make conversation. But with time, he blossomed. Now, it's one of his favorite parts of service. He's intentional about greeting every new man who walks through the door, making sure they feel seen and invited — just like he was.

That willingness to grow? That servant heart? That humility? It was the groundwork for everything that was to come.

And then came the moment that would shift everything. Not in him — he had already seen me. But in me.

It was November 3rd, 2024. I stood before the congregation and performed *"Look at God: A Test of Faith."* It wasn't just a spoken word piece. It was a prophetic outpouring, a release, a declaration of everything I had endured in the wilderness — and everything I was becoming. Will was there. Watching. Listening. Receiving. Something stirred in him that day. Something clicked. The veil began to lift — for him, and for me.

But that conversation — that moment where he actually approached me for the first time — is for the next chapter.

For now, just know this: the promise had already entered the room. He had already taken his seat. He had already started the work. The woman was waking up. The man was standing near. And heaven was holding its breath.

The test was almost over. The promise was about to speak.

CHAPTER 8:

Look at God – A Test of Faith

By the time Family Sunday arrived, I had gone three months without speaking to the Refining Forerunner. Three months of silence. Three months of aching, wondering, crying, detaching, reattaching, and then repeating that whole spiritual and emotional cycle again like it was a personality loop I couldn't break free from. I had mailed him an eight-page letter, poured out every broken piece of my heart—telling him how much it hurt to feel strung along, breadcrumbed, led into hope and left in limbo. My words were raw, layered in truth, longing, and confusion. I didn't know what kind of response, if any, I'd get. But I needed to say it.

It wasn't the first time I'd expressed myself like that. I'm a writer. It's how I process. It's how I collect my thoughts and make sure I'm not stumbling over feelings that deserve clarity. And every time I had opened up in writing before, he'd read my messages, acknowledged my pain, and yet… did nothing to change the narrative. Never invalidated me but never stepped up either. Like a man parked at the red light of our potential, foot hovering over the gas but refusing to drive.

After my birthday in July, the same week I quietly hoped he'd surprise me, show up, or at least acknowledge the day—I reached out to make plans. Just a little something, a dinner, a conversation, a chance to finally close the gap. But he told me point-blank that he couldn't give me what I needed. That even if he forced himself into a relationship with me at that moment, it wouldn't be right. And then he said something that made my heart twist in a new kind of ache: even if we weren't together, he still wanted and needed my friendship. Friendship? After everything we'd been through? After the emotional entanglement, the romantic declarations, the spiritual weight of our bond? We were never just friends. We dived headfirst into something deep, soul-binding, and messy from the start. And now he wanted to reduce me to a safe space he could still access—without the cost of commitment. The dagger came when I asked if he'd be jealous if he saw me with someone else, and he told me he wouldn't. That he just wanted me to be happy. Ouch. That was the moment I should've walked away for good. But instead, I wrote that letter—a final Hail Mary wrapped in revelation and grief.

And then I went quiet.

So by November, I was in a fragile place—healing but still hoping. Detached in spirit but faintly tethered in soul. A few weeks before Family Sunday, I broke the silence. I gave him a Starbucks gift card tucked inside a clergy appreciation card. It was small, but symbolic. A peace offering, maybe. An open door without fully walking through it. I didn't know what it meant yet—but I was testing the waters of closure or reentry. His birthday was also in November, and I had arranged to take him to dinner that same Sunday night after church. One last conversation. One last check-in. One last flicker of hope. I needed to know—really know—if there was anything left to salvage or if this was just divine closure dressed up in a salmon entrée and casual banter.

And listen, I already know what you're probably thinking. Sis… *why was it so hard to let go?* Why didn't I keep his number blocked, burn the letter, and move on with my life like a healed woman on TikTok telling strangers to "choose themselves"? I get it. But healing isn't linear, and hope is a stubborn little thing. When your heart's been cracked open by what felt like purpose, it's hard to accept when that purpose doesn't lead to partnership.

Let's rewind to the afternoon of that Family Sunday—because at Abundant Life, service starts at 3:15 p.m., not early morning like most churches. I showed up knowing the day carried weight. My nerves were electric. My spirit open but trembling. I had a spoken word piece to deliver—"*Look at God: A Test of Faith*"—but I also had layers of unfinished grief sitting in my chest. After worship, I stayed backstage while the rest of the worship team took their seats. I wanted to rehearse. Instead, I found myself in a tense conversation with God.

Not the soft kind. The real kind. The gritty, "Lord, this is not what we discussed" kind.

He was pressing me to go deeper. To say more than I rehearsed. To share what I had never said out loud in public spaces: my former marriage, my divorce, the depression that almost swallowed me whole, the slow rebuild of my faith and confidence, the detox from weed, cigar lounges, and empty relationships that left me hollow. He was calling me to peel back the curtain.

I resisted. "Sir… we did not go over this," I muttered in my spirit.

But He reminded me: *"You said yes. Back in May. This is the cost of that yes."*

As I stood trying to pull myself together, I heard clapping erupt in the sanctuary. Loud. Sustained. I panicked. Was I late? Did they already call my name?

I started making my way through the sanctuary when I passed Ms. Regina, seated in her usual spot near the back. Ms. Regina—heavyset woman who walks with a cane and carries the weight of spiritual wisdom like a crown—grabbed my hand with a smile and said, "You just got drawn for the blessing box, baby."

Every first Sunday, Abundant Life draws two names—a youth and an adult—to win a monetary gift as a surprise blessing.[33] God had pulled mine. It felt like a wink from heaven. A little holy encouragement. *"See? I see you. Now go say what I told you to say."*

And so I did.

When Pastor Dan called me to the stage, I stepped out in full obedience—and in a copper-brown, long-sleeved velvet dress. It hugged my curves with ruching around my belly, paired with chunky gold heels and gold accessories. I wasn't hiding my softness or my shine. I was showing up in full Leah mode. If you saw it, you better like it—because it wasn't going anywhere.

What was supposed to be an 8-minute piece became an 18-minute divine takeover. The Holy Spirit took the mic, and I just held on. I testified. I confessed. I edified. I declared that I was in a marriage season—even with no prospects in sight. That God was pruning me, preparing me, protecting me. I exposed the layers most people hide. And the altar call

---

33 Blessing Box: A monthly tradition at Abundant Life during Family Sunday where one adult and one youth are selected at random to receive a cash blessing and surprise from the church. It's both an encouragement and a reminder that God sees you—even when you're backstage negotiating with Him.

that followed? It was like floodgates opened. I had never seen such a response at our church before.

People came up to me afterward—men and women—saying how my transparency unlocked something in them. And somewhere in the crowd, a man named Will had been watching the whole time. I didn't think much of it in that moment. Not because I wasn't open—but because I wasn't looking. At least not for him. But that Sunday marked the first time I really *saw* him, too.

He waited for me in the foyer. Patiently. It had been over 45 minutes since service ended, and the sanctuary was nearly empty. When I finally stepped out, there he was—tall, bald, bearded, dressed in all black with a leather fur-lined jacket, mock neck, black slacks, and clean dress shoes. His beard was sharp. His smile was soft. His scorpion tattoo peeked down from his forearm toward his hand, and the neck ink peeking above his collar only added to the intrigue. It was giving… all the right things.

And he saw everything, too.

He approached with gentle confidence and told me I looked beautiful.

I said thank you.

And before I could stop myself—before I could even run it through a filter—I said, "Bald and bearded? That's sexy."

Yup. Out loud. In church. In the foyer. Post-sermon. It was like an intrusive thought that just jumped out—but baby, it landed. I saw that man stand a little taller. Smile a little deeper. He was feeling himself.

He started affirming me—talking about the weight of my words, the truth in my testimony. He shared glimpses of his own heartbreak, his desire for marriage and family, and how deeply my spoken word resonated with where he'd been. The way he opened up so quickly? It was disarming. Unexpected. Beautiful, even.

He told me he was 41. I was 31. I'd always imagined myself with an older man—seasoned, secure, but still learning. The kind of man who didn't need to be taught how to love, just encouraged to receive it. And there he was. But still, I didn't know what it all meant yet. Just that I saw him now. And he saw me.

After that powerful exchange, I went to dinner with the Refining Forerunner. Yep. Same day.

It was calm. Casual. I had planned it to celebrate his birthday. But underneath it all, I was testing the waters. I wanted to know if anything had changed. If he had changed.

I brought up that another man in the church seemed interested in me. I didn't say Will's name—but I wanted to see his reaction. He shrugged. Said it confirmed his good taste. Told me not to mention names because he was pretty sure he already knew who it was. I felt silly even bringing it up. Why did I think that would change anything?

We ate. We laughed. Then we got quiet. I asked him directly: "Why won't you choose me?"

He told me he couldn't give me what I needed. That he still had feelings. That I was beautiful. But that he wasn't ready. When I asked if he'd be jealous to see me with someone else, he admitted, "I would be. But I don't have a monopoly on Leah."

It landed like a thud.

And in that moment, I knew. He would never choose me. Not fully. Not freely.

So I chose myself. I didn't tell him about Will—not yet. But on the drive home, it was Will who occupied my thoughts.

And then came Egypt.

Pastor Dan had already told the whole congregation I was going. It was a 12-day trip with my mom that came together in a few weeks. Sweets was watching my dogs while I was gone. I had a stacked itinerary of pyramids, museums, and divine encounters lined up. Will had overheard the announcement at church and later told me Egypt had always been on his bucket list. He even had a tattoo of a pyramid from his pre-God days. He said he didn't love it anymore, but I told him it was part of his story.

Before I left, I knew I wanted to bring him something back. Just a small souvenir. A thank-you. A maybe.

I didn't have clarity about what we were. I wasn't even sure if anything would come of it. But something had shifted.

I finally saw him. The soft strength. The Godly confidence. The quiet pursuit.

And I was open.

The moment the promise started walking toward me in a black leather, fur-lined jacket and a soft smile, I didn't know what it meant.

But I knew what it wasn't.

It wasn't limbo.

CHAPTER 9

Love is in the Air – Acceleration Begins

*E*gypt was everything. Twelve days of divine whispers wrapped in ancient glory, jet lag, and luxury linens. Technically, two of those days were lost to flights and lay-overs, but the other ten? A full-blown, heaven-orchestrated itinerary of culture, clarity, and confirmation. From gliding down the Nile River on a dinner cruise to standing awe-struck before the Pyramids of Giza, it felt like I was walking through the pages of Scripture. I rode camels like a queen, touched the cool walls of tombs that had survived millen-nia, wandered the Egyptian Museum, and stood within the Library of Alexandria, breathing in the ancient wisdom my spirit seemed to crave.

But God didn't stop at monuments and hieroglyphics. He started talking — loudly.

Before we even landed in Cairo, I had a moment in the Istanbul airport that made my spirit sit up and take notice. As my mom and I waited near the food court, I saw this freestanding heart-shaped sign that read: "Love is in the Air." I froze. It felt like a divine billboard just for me. Not long before that, I had seen post after post in a Facebook group I was part of—one full of women believing for their kingdom marriage—sharing how they kept encountering that same exact phrase. And now here it was, staring me in the face in a Turkish airport, thousands of miles from home. Coincidence? I don't think so. My spirit sat up straight. My heart whispered, *pay attention*.

And just in case I thought it was a fluke, God repeated Himself. Days later, as the sun began to rise over Luxor and our hot air balloon inflated, flames roaring against the chilled desert air, I looked up… and there it was again. "Love is in the Air" printed boldly across the side of the balloon canvas. I ugly cried. Right there, surrounded by strangers, suspended between earth and heaven. God wasn't whispering anymore. He was hollering through helium and heat: *It's coming. It's close. Open your eyes.* [34] It felt like a heavenly wink, a reminder that God had not forgotten the promise. That love wasn't just on the way — it was airborne, elevated, and closer than I thought.

The trip itself was breathtaking. One of the most unforgettable moments was a rooftop photoshoot with the pyramids stretched behind me, ancient and unmoved. I wore a long, flowing red dress, the same image that would later inspire the cover of this book. At the time, I didn't realize Heaven was branding legacy into a photograph. I just knew I felt different. Set apart. Like I was stepping into a prophetic moment without fully understanding it yet. Looking back, it wasn't just a photoshoot. It was an unveiling. And when I came

---

34 *Isaiah 30:21 — "Whether you turn to the right or to the left, your ears will hear a voice behind you, saying, 'This is the way; walk in it.'"*

home, I didn't come back the same. I returned feeling powerful, chosen, and deeply aligned.

When I came home to Abundant Life, bag full of souvenirs for 25 people and a heart full of wonder, I wasn't prepared for what — or rather who — greeted me in the foyer. There stood Will, looking like he'd just stepped off the cover of GQ in a tailored burgundy suit, burgundy turtleneck, and a wide-brim black hat and black shoes to bring the full look together. He saw me rolling in with my overstuffed Hulken bag and opened his arms with a grin: "Welcome back, Cleopatra!" Sir. What?! That man had joy in his face just to see mine, and I didn't know what to do with it.

He was glowing. Not just smiling. Glowing. He immediately asked about my trip, demanded photo evidence on the spot, and joked about how jealous he was of my adventures. I was flattered… and flustered. And yes, there was a gift in my bag with his name on it — literally — but I panicked. I started passing out other gifts first, hoping he wouldn't see his name on one of the gift bags as I carefully shuffled things around. I didn't want to give it to him in front of everyone. Not yet.

It was Family Fellowship Sunday, our church's new tradition where we stayed after service for snacks and intentional connection. By the time I finished gift distribution and made it to the fellowship hall, most of the food was gone and the cleanup had started. Will was seated at a small table talking to another brother in Christ. Feeling bold, I asked, "Would you mind moving your Bible so I can sit here?" His face lit up like I'd just handed him a million dollars.

We sat there, in the middle of chaos and crumpled napkins, having what felt like a makeshift coffee date. My sister Ebonee sat nearby — unofficial chaperone, official eyebrow-raiser. Then Jessica sauntered past, leaned down, and whispered, "Girl, get your butt upstairs," with a knowing smirk. I pretended not to know what she meant, but let's be real — everybody saw it before I did.

Will and I talked about the spiritual family, his hopes for deeper brotherhood at church, how he longed for men to experience vulnerability the way women did. I was moved. Again. This man was different. He wasn't just saying stuff to sound deep. He meant it. It hit me in a place I didn't know needed attention.

And yet… I still didn't give him his gift.

When it was time to leave, he just gave me an awkward wave instead of a hug. He pulled back a bit, probably because we'd both mentioned how single folks at church often had eyes on them, and neither of us wanted to cause a scene.

But let me tell you—I couldn't sleep for two days. The Holy Spirit was nudging me so hard I felt like I was being spiritually poked in the forehead. Finally, I gave in. I reached out to the brother who first invited Will to church and asked for his number. (I said "Brother Will" in the most nonchalant tone like I wasn't feeling all the tension.) I texted him, letting him know I had something for him from Egypt and that I didn't give it to him because I felt nervous with so many eyes watching.

He responded kindly, saying he understood and didn't want anyone getting the wrong impression either. But of course, I had to go there. I crafted a clever little question, subtle but intentional—fishing for clarity in the way only a curious heart can. I needed to know if this was just surface-level kindness or if something deeper was stirring beneath the smile and scripture. His response? He said he was in a *season of transition*, focused on building godly friendships and growing in the Lord. *Cool story, bro.* I wanted more, but I respected the boundary. His texts started getting shorter, and I took the hint. So I bowed out gracefully—with my hope bruised, but my dignity fully intact.

The following week, a few of us decided to grab dinner after church — my WOW sisters: Andrene, Andrea, Shontee, and Caroline. It was an impromptu dinner at BJ's that Andrene initiated. When I realized Will and another brother were nearby, I invited them to join us. They came. Will sat right next to me. Didn't touch me, didn't flirt explicitly — but he did offer me a bite of his jambalaya and a sip of his cocktail. Just me. No one else. I filed that under: intriguing.

Midway through the meal, the conversation turned to kids. Everyone at the table had children except Will and me. He turned to me and asked, "Would you ever date a man with kids?" I gave the politically correct answer — "It depends on the man" — while internally screaming, "Absolutely not!" He smirked and said, "I have three kids." My face dropped. Internally, I crossed him off the list. But seeing my energy shift, he laughed and said, "I'm kidding! I don't have any." I almost threw a roll at him. But it was cute. And everyone could see it — the chemistry, the energy, the low-key flirting. I still pretended I didn't notice. Helen Keller energy.

A few days later, I floated the idea to our group chat: What if I hosted a New Year's Eve cocktail party followed by late-night bowling? Will's response came in hot. He was the first to reply, full of excitement and encouragement. But what really floored me? He didn't just support the idea — he immediately got to work behind the scenes. He called the bowling alley, spoke to the manager, booked the lane, paid the deposit — all without me asking. He texted me saying it was too much to explain via text and asked me to call him. That call? Supposed to be five minutes, ended up two hours. What started as logistics turned into laughter, banter, and a deepening connection. And I realized… I was in trouble. *The good kind.*

Then came Friday, December 20th — our next group outing: a movie night to see *Mufasa*. It was supposed to be a small co-ed group, but one of the brothers bailed last minute, leaving

Will as the only guy, along with me, and my sisters Ebonee and Andrea. He could've opted out too, but he didn't. He stayed and handled it with effortless grace. At one point, he even joked, "Y'all are making me look good—I feel like a king surrounded by all these beautiful women." And honestly? He did. Regal without trying. Present without posturing.

Midway through the film, he got up to refill the popcorn—for all the ladies, mind you—and the moment he disappeared down the aisle, Ebonee leaned in like the Holy Ghost had just given her clearance. "Sis… that's your husband," she whispered, dead serious. I nearly choked on my Mr. Pibb like it was communion and I wasn't worthy. "Girl, shut up," I hissed, smacking her arm as we kee-kee'd like teenagers trying to hold it together before he came back. But truth be told? She wasn't the only one sensing something.

And here's where it gets wild — the symbolism.

Mufasa wasn't born into royalty—but he was chosen. Scar had the lineage, but not the character. And in a way that only the Holy Spirit could orchestrate, it reminded me of Will. He didn't grow up in church. He wasn't a legacy Christian with a pedigree of pulpits behind him. But he had the oil. The reverence. The integrity. That rare, quiet strength that didn't need applause to be powerful. And the way he worshipped? Hands lifted, eyes closed, fully surrendered—week after week, without fail. [35] He carried his Bible like it was a sword, not a prop.[36] Served without needing a title. Pastor Dan had even called it out from the pulpit—how Will moved like a leader even without a mic in his hand.

What's wild is, long before I knew where this was heading—before I had clarity on who he would become to me—I was already moving prophetically concerning him. God kept highlighting things. Layers. Mantles. I could feel something being unearthed, revealed, stirred. I knew something was developing between us, but I didn't yet know what. Or why. All I knew was that the Lord was showing me pieces of his identity that he hadn't fully stepped into yet. I had already told him during one of our earlier conversations that he reminded me of Gideon—how Gideon questioned his worth and saw himself as the least, but God called him a mighty man of valor anyway. [37] And I saw the same in Will. A man in transition. A man unsure of his power. A man who needed someone to call it forth. He didn't have the bloodline. But he carried the mantle.

After the movie, Andrea and Ebonee conveniently had to go. Will and I weren't done. We went out for drinks and ended up closing the place down. It started light—movie commentary, inside jokes, playful banter. But somewhere between a laugh and a pause, the conversation shifted. The air got thick

---

35 *John 4:24* — "*God is spirit, and his worshipers must worship in the Spirit and in truth.*"
36 *Ephesians 6:17* — "*Take the helmet of salvation and the sword of the Spirit, which is the word of God.*"
37 *Judges 6:12* — "*When the angel of the Lord appeared to Gideon, he said, 'The Lord is with you, mighty warrior.'*"

with truth. I finally said what had been quietly brewing in my spirit for weeks: "I can't be spending time with a man whose intentions aren't clear." I laid it out plainly—his body language, the flirty undertones, the consistent presence. The energy had been loud, even if the words hadn't caught up yet.

He smirked, leaned back a little, and said, "Oh, you just gonna call me out like that?" And then came the line that shifted everything: "I guess it's time to put up or shut up." He reached for my hands, looked me directly in the eyes, and said with the gentlest, most disarming certainty, "I want to court you with the intention of making you my wife." It wasn't flashy. It wasn't rehearsed. It was steady. Sincere. Intentional. And the moment he said it, my spirit knew. It bore witness before my brain could catch up. Like something ancient in me stood at attention and whispered, *This is your husband, Leah.* And yet, even as my spirit was nodding yes, another part of me panicked. *Wait—am I actually ready for what I prayed for?* I tried to keep my face neutral, still, unbothered—so I wouldn't interrupt what God was doing in that moment. Because everything in me wanted to react, but I knew better. I didn't want to disrupt what heaven was orchestrating. I just listened. Held still. Let it wash over me.

He kept speaking—sharing how he had been watching me, praying about me, how God had shown him I was a wife… and he needed to find out if I was *his* wife. And right there, in the middle of a loud, crowded bar—with music playing, glasses clinking, and laughter echoing from nearby tables—the world around us blurred. All I could hear was the Holy Spirit: *Didn't you ask Me not to let you leave this year empty-handed? Look at your hands, Leah.* [38]And there they were—held in Will's. Steady. Covered. Full. I didn't know what the future

---

38 *Ecclesiastes 3:11* — *"He has made everything beautiful in its time. He has also set eternity in the human heart; yet no one can fathom what God has done from beginning to end."*

would hold, but I knew something real had just been spoken into existence. The promise wasn't just in the air anymore. It was sitting right across from me, grinning with intention.

Even after the bar closed, we weren't ready to leave. We walked outside and kept talking for nearly another hour in the parking lot—unpacking what had just happened, letting it sink in. And somewhere in that moment, I knew I had to be honest. All the way honest. So I told him everything. I told him about the Refining Forerunner. That we had history. That we had been intimate. I told him how long it lasted and why it lingered. Not to create drama, not to stir up shame, but because I had already lived the pain of being blindsided by someone's past through someone else's mouth. I didn't want that for Will. I didn't want him to be caught off guard by whispers or piecemeal truth—especially knowing we all went to the same church. He deserved to hear the full story from *me*, not the grapevine. I wanted him to have the dignity of making a fully informed choice about the future he was stepping into.

And he didn't flinch. He looked me in the eye and said, "I'm not worried about him. I got what you need." That moment floored me. There was no insecurity. No hesitation. Just presence. Confidence. Security. He stood there like a man who wasn't threatened—only sure of what he carried.

Before we left, we took our first photo together. He kissed me on the cheek, and I saved that moment as a marker. It wasn't about the picture—it was about what had just been planted. We drove off separately, but the conversation continued for several more hours on the phone. It was effortless, like something had clicked into place. And as the night faded into morning, I knew without question: *something had shifted. Something had begun.*

CHAPTER 10

God's Plan – From Courtship to Covenant

When God sets a covenant in motion, time bends to His will. What takes years for others can unfold in mere months when the Author of time Himself is writing the story. This wasn't infatuation, and it wasn't a performance. It was divine urgency—rooted in God's omniscience and wrapped in His mercy. The moment Will asked to court me, something in the Spirit shifted. It wasn't a rush to the altar—it was a summons to surrender. And we didn't force the pace. We simply followed His lead.

This chapter isn't just a love story. It's a month-by-month account of how God, in His infinite wisdom, accelerated what He had already settled in eternity. From December to May, we experienced the kind of divine momentum *Amos 9:13* points to—because heaven knew what was coming. God was mindful. Mindful of our hearts. Mindful of our pasts. Mindful of the strength we would need to endure what followed. And in His grace, He moved swiftly. Each month brought fresh revelation, deep conviction, and undeniable confirmation. This is how He brought us from courtship to covenant in under five months—not by chance, but by choice. His choice. No fluff. No fairy tale. Just favor, fire, and full surrender.

December — Awkward Photos, Honest Confessions, and the Kiss That Changed Everything

December 20th was the day Will officially asked to court me—right after we saw *Mufasa*. That moment was already sacred. But just a few days later, things took off like divine wildfire. On December 23rd, we came to church together, dressed with no prior coordination but clearly aligned in spirit. I wore a show-stopping red velvet, ruched dress—long sleeves, hugged curves, festive but classy. Will, wanting to match the moment, wore all black with a red bow tie and a shirt flecked with tiny red polka dots.

After service, we were standing near the Christmas tree in the foyer—a tall, grand tree that usually serves as the photo-op backdrop during the holidays. Sweets offered to take our photo. Normally, I'm a posing pro. I know my angles and exude confidence with a camera. But this time? I was nervous. *We* were nervous. You could *feel* the eyes on us. Pastor Carol was among those watching, and after our awkward little photoshoot, she came over, leaned in with a smirk, and said, "Let me see those pictures." I handed her my phone like a teenager caught in the act, and she simply nodded and said, "Y'all look cute." *Whew.*

We had no official plans for the day, but after church Will looked at me and said, "You look too good not to go show off. You wanna grab some food?" Flattered, I said yes. We headed toward the Tacoma Mall area, and I casually suggested Cheesecake Factory. He was stunned. Apparently, in the red pill/pink pill warzone of social media, Cheesecake Factory had become symbolic of low expectations. But I wasn't one of those women. I didn't need filet mignon to be impressed.

Still, God must've agreed with my dignity because when we walked in, we were ignored at the door and told there would be a 30–40 minute wait. Will wasn't having it. Without missing a beat, he redirected us next door to Texas de Brazil. Now, let me be clear—I wasn't used to being taken to fine dining restaurants by men with serious intentions. Temporary performers, sure. But a man with vision and follow-through? That was new. So I offered to split the bill. He shut it down immediately. "You keep your little money for casual stuff like bowling or movies. But this? You're not about to walk into a place like this, looking like that, and pull out your wallet." His masculinity was present and accounted for.

Over dinner, he started talking about our future like he was already my husband. He shared his passion for investments and financial literacy, how he wanted to build something sustainable, and how he saw money as a tool for legacy—not status. I could listen to him talk about finances all day. It wasn't just sexy—it was *stabilizing*. He spoke with authority and clarity, and I knew I wanted our future children to inherit that from him.

Meanwhile, I was turning heads all night. In Washington, even in upscale restaurants, people show up in athleisure. I walked in like a queen—and Will loved it. He didn't shrink. He sat tall, proud, and present. We ended up taking better photos that night at the restaurant—photos we still cherish as our first official couple shots.

But the real moment came after dinner. We sat in my car for nearly two hours, parked and wrapped in a tension that was both romantic and reverent. We kept repeating, "We don't wanna fall," trying to speak boundaries into the space between us. But somewhere in that pause, something deeper emerged. Will opened up his entire heart to me—raw, unfiltered, and trembling with truth. He told me things he wasn't proud of. Shared about his past—mistakes, insecurities, moments of brokenness that still haunted his confidence. He admitted the fears he carried about not being "enough" for a woman. Not the six-pack, six-figure, always-have-it-together man the world told him he needed to be. And he confessed that he worried no woman would want him if she knew the full picture.

But I did. And I was honored that he gave me a choice—to love the *whole* man, not just the polished version. His honesty didn't push me away—it pulled me in deeper. Because now I knew he wasn't hiding. Now I knew that he wanted to build something real.

Then, as if the moment couldn't carry more weight, he said, "I want you to hear this song." He played *Butta Love* by Next—a throwback I'd never heard before. As the lyrics filled the car, he sang along softly, his voice rich and vulnerable. I melted. The atmosphere was charged with something holy. And right there, in the front seat of my car, we shared our first kiss. Passionate. Electric. Covered in grace. And even though the fire had already been lit, we told each other goodnight—because we weren't trying to play with holy fire. We knew what we were carrying.

Christmas came next. I had no plans. No decorations. No expectations. Historically, the holidays had been lonely for me—just me and my fur babies, doing what we could to make it through. But Will made it his business to shift that narrative. He told me he'd be keeping his tradition of spending Christmas Eve with his mom but asked if he could spend Christmas Day with me. I said yes thinking it would be chill and low-key. What I wasn't expecting was a full-blown holiday miracle.

Despite the last-minute decision, Will somehow pulled together beautifully wrapped Christmas gifts—the kind of thoughtful wrapping you don't usually see from men. It wasn't just that he got me a Jimmy Choo perfume set and Gucci sunglasses—it was the heart behind it. The care in how he wrapped everything. The unspoken message that said, 'I see you, and I choose to show up. I didn't have anything to give him in return, and I told him that—but he looked at me, smiled, and said, "Your presence is gift enough." And I believed him.

We were hungry, but obviously it was Christmas Day, which meant our options were Denny's… or Chinese food. We chose Denny's—classic. After brunch, we stopped at a gas station to grab snacks for the movie marathon we had planned at my place. We didn't need anything fancy. Just each other.

When we got back, we settled in and started watching a movie, but barely paid attention. The love in the room was thick. The chemistry undeniable. At one point, he looked at me and said, "So… are you gonna say it?" He fished for it hard—and I tried to hold my ground—but eventually, I gave in. "I love you." He lit up. Gloated, of course. And then said it back. "I love you, too."

It was simple. Intimate. Sealed. And I knew in that moment—I was no longer walking through the holidays alone.

Then came New Year's Eve. I was hosting a cocktail party and had made a Costco run to grab some last-minute items. I was on the phone with Will while I shopped, asking for input on what else I should pick up—and that's when he started running his mouth. Teasing me. Saying I was probably about to serve everybody a whole bunch of store-bought stuff. "Honestly," he said, "I don't even know if you can really cook." Oh? *Bet.*

In his defense, every time he'd been over my place, my fridge had basically been empty. Maybe a few drinks, some snacks—but no evidence of home-cooked anything. But I was a single woman. If I wanted takeout, I got takeout. I didn't have anyone else to cook for, so I didn't feel pressed to be whipping up meals just to prove a point. But the way he was testing my gangsta? Yeah… it was time to show him what's up.

That night, I threw down: lemon herb grilled salmon, pan-seared garlic butter shrimp layered over creamy sour cream and chive mashed potatoes, with crispy brussels sprouts and bacon on the side. I didn't just cook—I made a statement. When he took his first bite, I saw it in his face. Shock. Gratitude. Conversion.

From that night forward, he started taking pictures of everything I made—documenting each plate like it was evidence in a wife-resume portfolio. Food is his love language, and I became fluent with cast iron, confidence, and just the right amount of seasoning.

At the party, people definitely started catching on. Jess, Kendie, and Caroline already knew about us, of course—they'd been riding shotgun through the early stages. But for everyone else, this night was the official unveiling. Our chemistry was undeniable. Obvious. And instead of awkwardness or side-eyes, we were met with head nods, warm smiles, and that quiet, collective *"Oh yeah… this makes sense."* It felt like we had the room's blessing without even having to ask for it.

But what made the night even more meaningful was the fact that this was the first time Will got to see me in my full element—hosting, designing, and rolling out the red carpet for my people. This wasn't just some cute little cocktail gathering. I *produced* this. From top to bottom. And it showed. I had curated a full spread with multiple appetizer stations: crispy pork belly and Brussels sprouts (a fan favorite), mashed potatoes with pot roast, baked brie with cranberry, cheese puff pastries, jalapeño chicken meatballs, and three themed cocktails—apple cider whiskey being the undeniable crowd favorite. And of course, Will made his homemade ceviche to contribute.

Themed desserts rounded everything out, and the entire night was drenched in warmth, connection, and intentional joy. He got to see my heart for hospitality—for loving people through food, aesthetics, and environment. And I got to experience what it felt like to be fully supported by a man who didn't need the spotlight to shine beside me. He was proud. Present. And all in.

As the night unfolded, you could literally feel the shift in the room. Couples who'd been together for years started leaning into each other more—hugging, holding hands, whispering in each other's ears. That fresh-love energy we carried? It was contagious.

We had made plans to go bowling afterward and Will had even put down a deposit. But we never made it. The party was too rich. Too full. Too *right*. When I mentioned the deposit, Will just shrugged and said, "That was an investment into my future." And the way he said it? I knew he meant every word.

— Revelation in Retrospect —

This was the month God let joy announce itself before certainty had a name. The blueprint was already unfolding — not with thunder or a prophetic dream, but with matching outfits, whispered affirmations, and the quiet arrival of a man who showed up with presence, not performance. I didn't need to be convinced. I just had to be still enough to receive. December wasn't just the start of us — it was the soft opening of answered prayer, proof that God remembers even the ache of the holidays and sends redemption in velvet and ceviche.

January — Family Fellowship, The Towing Fiasco, and Finding My Voice Again

January came in with weight and glory. The first Sunday of the month, I led my first Family Fellowship Hour at church—which also doubled as our nine-year anniversary celebration. It was my first official assignment after being appointed church event coordinator, and let me tell you: it was no small task. I had never cooked for more than 16 people.

But that day, I planned for 40 to 50 and ended up feeding between 60 and 70.

The menu was simple: baked spaghetti, cajun penne pasta, a salad bar, dessert, and punch. But God multiplied that food like the two fish and five loaves. The compliments came pouring in—folks couldn't stop talking about how good the food was. Even Pastor Dan didn't know I was the one who cooked until someone else told him. Some people even asked why I didn't just cater the event with the church budget—I hadn't realized that was an option. But it didn't matter. I served with excellence. And God honored it.

That same day, Kristal—yes, the very same Kristal who had prophesied over me back in May 2024—was at church for her sister's book signing. She hadn't seen me since that prophetic encounter. When she spotted me sitting beside Will, she looked at me and said, "Girl… is that your husband?" I was like, "No… we just started courting, like two weeks ago." But she knew. She pulled us both aside and prophesied over Will. She called him out—read him for absolute filth in the Spirit. She spoke to his abandonment wounds, his orphan spirit, his comparison issues, his deep insecurities about not being "enough," and even the weight of ministry that wouldn't look like traditional church.

He didn't say a word. Just held my hand tightly while she spoke. That moment marked something pivotal for both of us. God was confirming through someone *completely* outside our relationship the very things He had only revealed to me.

And then came the towing saga. One night, Will came over, and I reminded him—as I always did—to park in my carport. The parking situation at my complex is tight, and I didn't want him to get towed. But, being a man, he brushed it off. Later that night, I took the dogs out and noticed he wasn't parked in my space, but it was raining and dark, so I didn't clearly see where he'd parked.

We fell asleep on the couch. The next morning, I looked outside—and his car was gone. I instantly knew. He had parked in a loading zone that blocked another resident's carport. His car had been towed in the middle of the night.

He was devastated. He immediately said, "I'll just pay it." But it was a weekend—and the fee was over $620. I told him to wait. Because of my past experience in property management, I had a connection with the tow company's owner. I spent the entire day making calls, calling in every favor I had. And by the grace of God, I got his car released for free.

Will was stunned. Grateful. And I learned something powerful that day too: I had been so conditioned in my previous marriage to silence myself, to hold back my voice, even when I knew I was right. I saw him park wrong, and I said nothing. Because I didn't want tension. But God showed me: Will wasn't my past. I didn't have to shrink or stay silent. My voice mattered. My discernment mattered. And I was finally learning to trust it again.

— Revelation in Retrospect —

This month wasn't just about feeding people — it was about realizing what I carried. God used pasta, prophecy, and even a parking mishap to remind me that I was no longer the silenced version of myself. I wasn't just stepping into love; I was stepping into leadership. January taught me that my voice had weight, my wisdom had value, and my obedience could open doors no key could. This wasn't just a courtship — it was a classroom. And I was finally showing up to class as me.

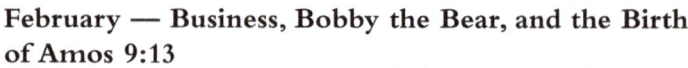

February — Business, Bobby the Bear, and the Birth of Amos 9:13

February ushered in favor. Will began to speak into my purpose in ways I didn't know I needed. He challenged me to stop treating my design business like a side hustle. He told me, "People are going to start noticing you—and you need to be ready. You need to be charging what you're worth."

That encouragement turned prophetic. A referral partner sent me a last-minute wedding: 150 guests. Only three weeks to plan and execute. I wasn't sure I could pull it off. But Will said, "I'll help you every step of the way."

And he did. Will supported me every step of the way.

The wedding was scheduled for Saturday, February 1st, and the night before, we put in *thirteen straight hours* transforming the reception hall. When I say the space was rough—I mean *rough*. The walls were hideous. The stage was cluttered with junk, being used more like storage than a platform. It needed a total revival. But I saw the vision in my head, and Will matched my energy from the moment we walked in.

When I'm in work mode, I can get a little intense. Focused. Direct. Sometimes that tone softens when I remember to say "please" and "thank you," and other times it doesn't. But Will didn't flinch. Didn't fold. Didn't make me feel like I needed to be small just to be tolerated. He followed my lead with grace, with patience, and with an unwavering "I got you."

We didn't get out of that venue until around 3 or 4 in the morning. Barely enough time to blink. So we did what we could—drove home for a quick nap, showered, and then turned right back around just a few hours later. We still had to decorate the sanctuary for the ceremony itself, because the night before we'd only had enough time to focus on the reception. It was the kind of setup that demanded everything from you, and then some.

After the ceremony, we didn't even leave. We were *so* exhausted that we ended up crashing in the back of the U-Haul. Cold. Wet. No insulation. Just two bodies layered in tiredness, laying flat on sacrifice. We waited there until the ceremony ended so we could tear down the sanctuary decor, haul it downstairs, and repurpose it for the reception setup.

And still… Will didn't complain. Not once. He didn't side-eye me, didn't act like I owed him for anything. He stayed present. Steady. Holding me down through every grunt, every chill, every silent moment in that freezing truck. He didn't just show up for me—he *covered* me. And in that moment, I remember looking over at him and thinking: *This man really loves me.* He took it like a G. A gentle one. A God-sent one.

The event turned out stunning. The transformation was undeniable. The content I got for my design portfolio was next-level—and the bookings started rolling in not long after. All because Will didn't just believe in me. He *dared* me to take myself seriously. He spoke life into my calling. He stood in the trenches with me.

And somewhere between the late-night U-Haul naps and the final flip of the reception hall, I started to realize—I wasn't just falling in love. I was witnessing revival.

Then one night, while we were on the phone for our usual 6–7 hour call, he said, "Things between us are happening so fast, I can't keep up." Instantly, the Holy Spirit dropped Amos 9:13 into my spirit. I couldn't remember where it was exactly, but I knew the Word said something about blessings overtaking you. I Googled the phrase—and there it was:

"Yes indeed, it won't be long now. Things are going to happen so fast your head will swim…"

We both felt it. That became our foundational scripture. We declared it. We confessed it. We held onto it. Because we knew—this was only the beginning.

Valentine's Day rolled around, and to be honest, I wasn't sure if I was even going to see Will. He had just started a new job and didn't want to rock the boat by asking for time off too soon, so I had already braced myself for the possibility that the day might come and go quietly. But to my surprise, he made sure I felt loved. Seen. Celebrated. Something I hadn't felt on Valentine's Day in years.

He showed up with beautiful flowers, a box of chocolate-covered strawberries, and a teddy bear named Bobby—all from Edible Arrangements. The kind of sweet, curated bundle that said, *"I thought of you."* He only had about an hour and a half to spare before heading into a long overnight shift, but he gave me *all* of that time with his full presence. No rush. No distractions. Just us.

We curled up on the couch and watched *The Chosen* together. I nestled under his arm, tucked into a quiet warmth that didn't need words to be profound. It wasn't extravagant. But it was *perfect*. And even though he had to leave for work, I didn't feel abandoned. I felt cherished. Because love doesn't have to be loud to be *real*.

March — Conviction, Confession, and Ring Shopping

March brought the fire—literally and spiritually. Despite our best efforts to abstain, we fell. And it broke us. Not because we didn't love each other, but because we *did*. Deeply. Truly. Intensely. We were convicted. Both of us wanted to honor God. We knew this relationship carried weight, and we wanted to walk it out in a way that was pleasing to Him. But it was hard—harder than we imagined.

Neither of us had ever been in a relationship that felt this safe, this soul-affirming, this naturally intense. Being near one another gave us peace. Comfort. A kind of spiritual security that neither of us had experienced before. But that same closeness made abstinence feel nearly impossible. We weren't rushing to get married just so we could have sex—we were already talking about forever. But we also couldn't deny that we were struggling to surrender our flesh while the spirit was crying out to be obedient. It was that *Matthew 26:41* moment: *"The spirit is willing, but the flesh is weak."* [39]

So, we started having real conversations about marriage. Timelines. Readiness. Summer seemed realistic. But I admitted—I wasn't sure I could wait that long. Not because

---

39 *Matthew 26:41 (NIV) – "Watch and pray so that you will not fall into temptation. The spirit is willing, but the flesh is weak."*

I didn't trust God, but because the desire was so strong, and our bond so magnetic, that even distance didn't feel like protection anymore. It felt like torment.

Will responded in the most beautiful way—he took me ring shopping. And when I say he paid attention? He took *notes.* I changed my mind at least five times, but he caught every detail, every preference, every sparkle in my eyes. I knew— whenever he proposed, he'd get it right. I started showing pictures to my sister circle, trying to act like I was calm. But my heart was already picking out playlists.

We also knew that not everyone would celebrate us. Some would genuinely rejoice. Others would struggle with it. We were aware that the mantle of kingdom marriage came with both *favor and friction.* But none of that mattered more than our obedience. We didn't just want each other—we wanted God's blessing over us. And we were finally starting to understand what it would cost.

— Revelation in Retrospect —
March taught us that conviction isn't condemnation — it's a call to alignment. We weren't failing because we didn't care. We were fighting because we did. Our love wasn't casual, and neither was the calling on it. The fire exposed our humanity, but it also revealed our hunger for holiness. And in the midst of weakness, God whispered clarity. Ring shopping wasn't about rushing — it was about readiness. We weren't just dreaming of covenant. We were counting the cost.

April — Dreams, Discipline, and Ephesians 5:31

April didn't come with noise. It came with a dream. On April 6th at exactly 5:31 a.m., I woke up from what felt like a divine visitation—heart racing, spirit stirring, the kind of vivid revelation that leaves no room for doubt. In the dream, Will and I were laying up together, and at some point, he

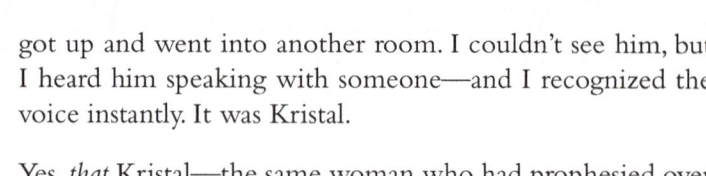

got up and went into another room. I couldn't see him, but I heard him speaking with someone—and I recognized the voice instantly. It was Kristal.

Yes, *that* Kristal—the same woman who had prophesied over me almost a year earlier, calling forth my destiny with surgical precision. And just like before, her words in the dream carried the same weight, accuracy, and heaven-breathed urgency.

In the dream, she entered the bedroom where I was but then turned to leave. Will and I followed her outside to the parking lot to finish the conversation. That's when she shifted into a prophetic state and began to speak—first to Will.

She said, "It's time to marry. No procrastination. No questions about provision. God said to get it done. And don't worry about the money."

Then she turned to both of us and continued, "God has given you everything you need for a small wedding."

She paused again, visibly listening for more from the Lord. I could feel what was coming and instinctively turned my face. The last time Kristal had spoken into my life prophetically, she called out everything I thought I was hiding—and I wasn't trying to go through that again. But the word came anyway.

She looked at us both and said, "God knows about the sex—and it does not honor Him. No more sex until you're in covenant. He wants to bless your obedience and sacrifice."

Will immediately agreed and said he'd been thinking the same thing. I agreed too—because I knew obedience was better than sacrificing the blessing. Then Kristal slipped right back into silence. After a few seconds, she came out of the

Spirit and simply walked away. Will and I locked eyes. We didn't speak. We didn't have to. We both knew.

When I woke up, it felt like I was returning from a real-life conversation. The Holy Spirit urged me to write it all down immediately in my phone. And when I checked the time—5:31 a.m.—I felt that nudge to look up *Ephesians 5:31*. When I did, it broke me:

"For this reason a man shall leave his father and mother and be joined to his wife, and the two shall become one flesh." [40]

As I was still typing in my Notes app, Will suddenly gasped in his sleep. Loud. Startling. I turned to him and asked if he was okay—if he'd been dreaming too. He said no. But I *knew* something spiritual was happening. His spirit was clearly connected to what I had just experienced. You can't convince me otherwise.

We didn't talk about it in that moment. I just said, "Let's talk when we're actually awake." He nodded and went back to sleep. But later that morning, when we were both up for real, he asked me about it. I told him everything. And he received it instantly. No pushback. No defensiveness. Just full agreement.

And let's be real—what man, in the thick of new love and real desire, says *no* to sex unless he's being led by the Spirit? Exactly. Even the Spirit-led ones still struggle. So for him to say yes to obedience that fast? That wasn't just conviction. That was covenant-level submission. That was God.

Oh, and for anyone reading this thinking it sounds too wild or too cinematic to be true—don't worry. I've still got

---

40 *Ephesians 5:31 (NKJV) – "For this reason a man shall leave his father and mother and be joined to his wife, and the two shall become one flesh."*

the note saved in my phone. Timestamped and untouched. Receipts stay ready.

— Revelation in Retrospect —

April brought clarity—but not closure. The dream was unmistakably God. The word was corrective, convicting, and undeniable. And while we both received it with open hearts, what we didn't receive was a timeline. That part? It stretched us. Obedience without a clear "when" will humble you quick. But still—we said yes. Because even when the road ahead felt uncertain, we knew what was at stake. We weren't just chasing a wedding. We were choosing covenant, even in the waiting.

May — A Trunk Full of Faith and a 24-Hour Covenant

May didn't stroll in—it hit like a divine deadline. Everything God had whispered, confirmed, and stirred was suddenly pushing to the surface. And I felt it in my body. My spirit. My trunk.

It started on May 3rd, when Will and I stopped by K&G to grab a few things for our upcoming trip to Mexico. It was supposed to be a casual shopping trip for vacation clothes, but while we were browsing, he spotted a dusty pink tuxedo jacket with intricate embroidery—and lit up. He's always been drawn to soft, pastel tones. I'm more of a bold, vibrant color girl. If it had been up to me, I would've gone for bright florals and a springtime wedding. But back in March, when we started seriously talking about marriage, Will had mentioned "maybe summer," so I adjusted my expectations accordingly.

That day, we bought the jacket and a pair of black rhinestone-covered shoes to match. He already had black pants, so I didn't stress about tuxedo pants with the satin stripe. But I mentally clocked that he still needed a tuxedo shirt and a bowtie. At the time, I had no idea we'd be getting married ten days later—but God did.

Then came Friday, May 9th—WOW Life Group night. At the end of the session, Jessica released a prophetic word: "God is going to ask someone in this room to do a hard thing this week." I nodded like amen, but deep down, I didn't think it was for me. I was already carrying so much—emotionally clogged, spiritually heavy, and unsure how to even put language to what I was feeling. I wasn't expecting God to add anything else to my plate. But He was about to.

As usual, after group ended, we lingered in the parking lot. Because parking lot ministry always hits different. We stay back to kee kee, laugh, cry and let the Spirit move however it wants to. Sometimes it's lighthearted. Other times, it turns into divine surgery with no anesthesia. That night was a mix of both.

Prophetess had been at group with us, but she decided to stay for the afterglow. Now let me describe her properly. This woman carries an apostolic anointing with a prophetic edge sharp enough to slice through pride, confusion, or spiritual apathy in a single word. One minute she's got you doubled over in laughter, and the next she's staring into your soul, delivering a *thus saith the Lord* that you can't shake. Loud and loving. Playful and precise. The kind of woman who'll say what everyone else is too scared to—and back it up with receipts from heaven. We always say, *"It's giving flexibility."*

That night, the jokes shifted into conviction. She looked at me and said, "Y'all need to get married. If he goes to Mexico with you and y'all aren't in covenant, y'all are gonna fall into a pool of sin. Wouldn't you rather please the Lord?"

I told her I was ready. And I meant it. I had the dress, the shoes, the accessories—all the things. But I also admitted I didn't want to be the one to bring it up to Will. I didn't want to pressure him. As much as I felt the weight of what God was saying to *me*, I wanted Will to hear it for *himself*. I wanted him to move not because I nudged—but because God stirred. That mattered to me. I had initiated too much in past relationships. This time, I needed to see God lead the man. I didn't want my obedience to become manipulation.

So I told them I was ready… but quiet. And then, I shared the dream—the one from early April that had rocked me to my core. Kristal had appeared, speaking prophetically with clarity and fire. I didn't need to rehash every word; just bringing it up stirred the urgency all over again. I explained how I had woken up at exactly 5:31 a.m., how Will—sleeping beside me—suddenly gasped as I was recording it in my phone. And how, when I told him about it later, he didn't flinch.

He received it like his spirit had already said yes. That dream marked a shift in both of us. And as I stood there retelling it, I could feel that same conviction settling in again like fresh oil.

After I shared it, Prophetess looked at me again and said, "Well then, stay ready so you don't have to get ready. Keep everything in your trunk. If that man calls an audible, you don't want to be caught off guard."

It sounded wild. I laughed it off at first. But later that night, I did exactly what she said.

When I got home, I opened Amazon Prime and ordered a tuxedo shirt and rhinestone bowtie for Will—next-day shipping. They arrived the next evening, Saturday, May 10th. I stayed up late that night ironing his shirt, pressing my dress, organizing our shoes and accessories, putting everything in garment bags and neatly laying them in my trunk. I even arranged it in a way where if Will happened to go to my car, he wouldn't notice. The man had no idea I was driving around with a whole wedding packed and ready. It felt insane. It was crazy faith, and I knew it. But I also knew God was preparing something.

And in my mind, I thought *maybe the audible would be called at church*. We had talked about possibly getting married at Abundant Life before. I didn't know how it would unfold. But I was staying ready.

Sunday, May 11th came. I told Will I'd be wearing black and white and asked him to do the same. Not because I wanted us to be cute and matchy-matchy, but because I knew it would guarantee he wore black pants—the final piece of the tuxedo look. He didn't need tuxedo pants with a satin stripe. Black was enough. I was moving in silence—but ready. I wanted to be sure that *if* God moved, there'd be nothing missing. No scrambling. Just covenant, on call.

But the day came and went—and nothing happened.

We went home separately that night, and I was heavy. I didn't say anything, but I was grieving silently. The urgency in my spirit hadn't lifted. I just didn't know what else to do.

Then came Monday, May 12th.

Will called me to check in. He could tell I was off and kept pressing gently until I finally opened up. I told him everything. That I wanted to get married. That I couldn't carry this burden much longer. That I didn't need an engagement or a proposal or a party—I just needed obedience.

At first, he was surprised. A little frustrated. "What do you mean skip the engagement?" That's when he revealed that he had already purchased my engagement ring. It was being shipped to Jared's, needed to be resized, and then picked up. He was planning to propose at the end of the month after our Mexico trip. He had been working with Jessica behind the scenes to make it special for me.

When he said it, I felt a wave of emotion—honored, moved, a little heartbroken, but mostly grateful. It told me everything I needed to know: his heart had been in the right place all along. But I also knew where God was leading me.

So I said, "As beautiful as that would be… I'd rather be in covenant. This is about alignment. Obedience. Saying yes to the season—not the spectacle."

He got quiet—not unsure, just reverent. And after a pause, he said, "If you're sure… then let's do it."

Just like that, we started calling our people. And without hesitation, every single one of them said yes. No delays. No questions. No shock. It was as if heaven had already briefed them, and they were just waiting for us to pull the trigger.

The next day, Tuesday, May 13th, we got married.

It was a quiet park with a dock by the lake. The trees moved like they'd been waiting for us. There was no rehearsal. No performance. Just peace. Just presence.

Our inner circle gathered—those who had walked with us, prayed for us, and seen the promise forming. Pastor Dan and Pastor Cheryl joined via FaceTime, and Jeff, though unable to leave work on such short notice, was with us in spirit. Everything we needed was there. Covenant was the only agenda.

Jessica made our playlist, brought the Martinelli's, and served as my flower girl. Caroline picked up the bouquet. Pastor Carol brought the broom. Pastor J handled the certificate and vows. I designed the signage and backdrop. It was simple, beautiful, and exactly what heaven intended.

Two days later, we flew to Mexico.

We thought we were heading to a destination wedding… and instead, we stepped into our honeymoon. Just like that. It was surreal. The suite was two stories with a rooftop jacuzzi and stunning views. We laughed hard—deep belly laughs that felt like freedom. We zip-lined, rode ATVs, and even went horseback riding. It was Will's first time on a horse, and yet he was a natural. Confident, calm, connected. I had never seen him so free. The whole trip was adventure, rest, intimacy, joy. It felt like we had stepped into another world. It was the most joy we'd experienced in such a concentrated amount of time. Just peace. Just us. Just God's hand.

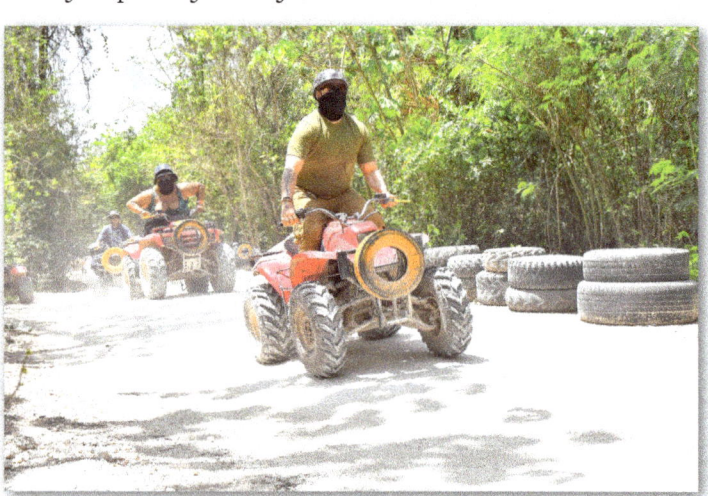

And more than anything, it felt like redemption.

On my first honeymoon years ago, I flew to the destination alone. My former spouse missed the flight and left me hanging. I was heartbroken and embarrassed—forced to step into what should've been a celebration by myself. It was a dark start to what became a deeply painful union.

But this time? I arrived with my husband. I was chosen. Covered. Protected. I felt God whispering, *"This is how I redeem what was stolen. This is how I restore what was lost."* [41]It wasn't just a honeymoon—it was a holy do-over. It was beauty for ashes, joy for mourning, and a divine promise kept. [42]

But the joy didn't last as long as we expected. We didn't know we'd be returning to sorrow.

On May 22nd, just one week after our wedding, Will's mother passed away.

Suddenly, everything made sense. The urgency. The dreams. The pressing from heaven that wouldn't let up. God hadn't been rushing us for romance. He had been positioning us for reality.

Will didn't need a girlfriend. He didn't need a future fiancée.

He needed a wife. An intercessor. A partner to walk him through grief and not run from it. A covenant that could withstand the weight of real life.

And by God's grace, I was already in position.

This chapter ends with joy, loss, and the mystery of divine timing. We accelerated into covenant... only to accelerate into bereavement. But even that was part of the blueprint. Because when God builds something, He doesn't just plan the promise—He prepares for the storm.

---

41 Joel 2:25 (NIV) – *"I will repay you for the years the locusts have eaten—the great locust and the young locust, the other locusts and the locust swarm—my great army that I sent among you."*

42 Isaiah 61:3 (NKJV) – *"To console those who mourn in Zion, to give them beauty for ashes, the oil of joy for mourning, the garment of praise for the spirit of heaviness; that they may be called trees of righteousness, the planting of the Lord, that He may be glorified."*

We had said yes to each other. And now, we would find out what that yes would cost.

— Revelation in Retrospect —

May felt like a contradiction. I had just come out of a wilderness—the year-long refining season that nearly broke me—and finally stepped into what I believed was the promise. But instead of rest, I was met with rupture. It didn't feel like fulfillment. It felt like another breaking. I didn't expect to trade wedding joy for unexpected loss.

I could see how covenant became Will's covering—how it gave him the space to grieve, to shut down, to feel what he needed without pressure. But for me? It felt like there was no room to fall apart. No room to process the emotional whiplash of joy turning into mourning. And deep down, I wrestled with a question I didn't know I was allowed to ask: "What does a grieving husband give to me?" I felt robbed. Rushed. Cheated out of my celebration season.

What God was asking of me wasn't just to say yes to marriage— He was asking me to say yes to surrender. To trust His timing over my expectations. To choose covenant even when it came cloaked in pain. He was asking, "Will you walk into purpose, even when it doesn't look like the promise you pictured?" And somehow… even in the confusion, I obeyed. I didn't feel ready. But I was chosen. And I was built for this.

CHAPTER 11:

The Space Between – Bleeding Promises & Bruised Expectations

Will used to say his prophetic number was 11. That God would often speak to him through it—on clocks, addresses, license plates. And while I never fully grasped the significance, I did notice something oddly fitting when I realized this would be Chapter 11. The space between what was promised and what's painfully being lived. The space between the altar and the after. The tension of the in-between.

We got married on May 13th. 5 + 1 + 3 = 9. A number of acceleration. It was our Amos 9 moment—when heaven moves quickly and alignment falls into place. But just nine days later, we came home from our honeymoon, and Will found his mother lifeless on the couch. May 22nd. 5 + 2 + 2 = 9. Another acceleration. Only this time, it wasn't breakthrough. It was bereavement. The same number that once marked covenant now marked crushing. Two accelerations, both real—one wrapped in joy, the other in sorrow.

She had been gone for a couple of days by the time we found her. The moment still replays in my mind. Him running outside, collapsing in my arms, screaming, "She's dead!" Me holding him while trying to hold myself together. We were barely two weeks into marriage and already knee-deep in trauma. And after that? It felt like everything unraveled.

I tried to be supportive. To hold space for his grief. To cook, to clean, to pray, to plan. I didn't get to meet his mother in person, something I had asked for many times before our wedding—but he had his reasons, I guess. Still, her death marked a turning point. Not just in his life, but in ours.

He started slipping jabs into conversations—accusations disguised as observations.

"You sleep all day."
"You don't cook."
"I come home to leftovers and a dirty floor."
"You don't want to work."
"You just wanted a wedding, not a marriage."

Words like daggers. And because words of affirmation are my love language, each one sliced deep. I would try to explain how deeply it affected me, but his response would be clinical:

"If it's not true, why are you so hurt?"
"The best version of you is your responsibility."
But even if it's not true, even if it's twisted—if it's coming from your husband, it still wounds.

What he didn't see was everything I actually did do. I organized our entire home after he moved in, when his boxes were stacked in the living room like a fortress. I made space. I set up the closet. I folded his clothes. I created a home for both of us. I cooked, I cleaned (maybe not every day, but often), I did all the grocery shopping and meal planning, took care of the dogs, supported ministry events, kept applying for jobs despite my work trauma, and still managed to show up in our church community. But somehow, in his eyes, it was never enough. I wasn't enough.

We were supposed to be partners. Covenant. "We" not "me." But I was constantly made to feel like I was slacking, like my contributions were invisible. And whenever I voiced my pain or tried to share my experience, I was told I wasn't taking accountability. That I only ever said "you make me feel" instead of "we're struggling." But how do you share something that feels one-sided without telling the truth of your side?

I've been blamed for the cracks in our communication—while being the only one actively trying to mend them. And when I don't reconcile the way he wants, or respond with instant enthusiasm, I'm accused of not caring enough about our marriage. But I'm not a robot. I can't switch emotional gears on command.

I'm tired. And this is where it gets real.

Because I look around and I see women in the world—women who live by their own rules, post what they want, dress how they want, prioritize their careers and pleasures—and they seem to be thriving. They have husbands who adore them publicly and accept them wholly. Women who aren't weighed down by religious expectations or afraid of losing themselves in the process of trying to be "a good wife." And I ask God: Why does it seem like they get to be free while I feel imprisoned in what's supposed to be a promise?

And yet… I don't want their life. I want the one I was promised. But I also want to feel loved in it. Covered in it. Safe in it.

I'm not asking for perfect. I'm asking for effort. I'm asking for consistency. For conversation that builds instead of breaks. For affection that isn't a reward for compliance. For the kind of love that mirrors Christ and His bride[43].

---

43 *Ephesians 5:25* — *"Husbands, love your wives, just as Christ loved the church and gave himself up for her."*

The irony? I still believe in the promise.
But the promise is bleeding.
And I'm bruised by expectation.

There's a saying: a woman multiplies what she's given.
Give her a seed—she gives you life.
Give her a house—she makes it a home.
Give her consistency—she'll give you legacy.
But give her criticism—she will drown in self-doubt.
Give her silence—she will question her worth.
Give her coldness—she will become guarded.
Give her crumbs—and she will still try to bake bread with it, until the starvation hollows her out.
I am that woman.
I multiply what I'm given. But I am no longer ashamed of asking for something worth multiplying.

I'm not writing this to tear down my husband. I'm writing this because I made a vow not to lose my voice again. I lost it in my first marriage. I silenced myself into a depression so deep I barely clawed my way out. I won't do it again. Not even for a man I love.

This chapter isn't a funeral. It's a witness.
A witness to the tension between obedience and grief.
A witness to a covenant that hurts.
A witness to promises that don't look like what you expected.
A witness to love trying to survive a storm it didn't see coming.

We're still in the space between.
And this is what the space looks like.

But let me be clear: there have also been good days. Moments of light cracking through the heaviness. In the time since I began writing this chapter, I've seen the Lord begin to turn things around. The warfare was so intense, I had to pause writing—because I was living in the trenches. There were days I didn't even feel called to finish this book. How could I call this a promise when all I felt was pain?

I see it clearer now. Sometimes, God will test your love for the promise—not to destroy it, but to see if you trust Him more than the thing He gave you. Just like Abraham and Isaac. The promise still had to go to the altar. Why? Because even the promise can become an idol.

It's not that I was idolizing marriage. It's that God was calling me to deeper obedience. And obedience will always cost you comfort.

Abraham waited decades for Isaac. Just like I waited years to be married again. And now, God was asking me to do the same thing Abraham did: give the promise back to Him. Give Will back to Him. This wasn't about sacrifice. It was about surrender.

Marriage, at its core, is sanctifying. It will purify you. Expose you. Stretch you. Heal you. Break you down—and build you up again, not in your strength, but in God's. And even in the darkest moments—when I wanted to give up—I had to believe that God could still do a work in Will. That the man I married in transition is still the man God chose for me.

Because faith that moves God doesn't make sense. By faith Abraham, when God tested him, offered Isaac as a sacrifice… Abraham reasoned that God could even raise the dead—and so in a manner of speaking, he did receive Isaac back from death[44]. That's crazy faith. And that's the kind of faith I'm choosing. Even here. Even now. In the space between.

---

44 Hebrews 11:17–19 — "By faith Abraham, when God tested him, offered Isaac as a sacrifice… Abraham reasoned that God could even raise the dead—and so in a manner of speaking, he did receive Isaac back from death."

— Revelation in Retrospect —

After reflecting on the tension of the space between, I now see how God was working behind the scenes in ways I couldn't understand in the moment. Will's hurtful words came from places of deep fear— fear that I didn't see him, fear that I didn't honor him as the man of our house. His insecurities were being plagued by the enemy, and the devil knew exactly where to attack. The fear became so loud, it manifested as pride and a refusal to take accountability. But I prayed. I prayed for God to restore my husband, to bring him back to the man I married—the man I believed in, even in the midst of his grief and struggle. And God answered. Will has since admitted that he was acting out of his own fear, not because of me. He's taken accountability, and I've seen real change. He's covered me in ways I didn't expect. The apology wasn't just words—it was backed by changed behavior. And I know now that this was part of God's acceleration in our relationship. The kind of quick work He promised in Amos 9:13, even through the hardest moments.

CHAPTER 12

A Chosen Leah – Marked by Obedience, Mantled for Legacy

Twelve. The number of divine government. Completion. Fullness in God's timing. It's no coincidence this is the final chapter. Just as twelve sealed the foundation of tribes, apostles, and heavenly order, so does it seal this book—not as an ending, but a coronation. The completion of one journey and the commissioning into the next.

I didn't write this because I wanted to. I wrote it because I was *yielded*. That's the revelation the Lord gave me: that He entrusted me with this mantle not because I was the most qualified, but because I said yes. Because I surrendered. Because I made myself available. It was the yes that unlocked the assignment. And that's where Esther comes in.

When Mordecai told her, "If you remain silent at this time, relief and deliverance will arise from another place," something in her shifted. Esther didn't feel ready. She didn't feel righteous enough. But the moment demanded her voice. She didn't ask to be highlighted, but heaven called her to the forefront. I didn't want to be a public display of process either. I didn't want to relive the trauma, the divorce, the poor decisions, the refining fire, or the warfare in my promise. But God saw a yielded vessel. He saw a woman who would surrender her comfort for the sake of her calling. And He chose me for such a time as this. [45]

I said yes, and that yes became the soil for legacy.

This book is not about marriage. Not really. Marriage was the frame, but the canvas is so much bigger. This is about the refinement of a woman. The sanctification of a prophetic voice. The restoration of a daughter. This is about the making of a mantle. This is about covenant—yes, in marriage, but also in sisterhood, in spiritual community, in identity, in calling, and most of all, covenant with God.

It's not lost on me that in the process of writing this, God kept allowing me to minister to women navigating similar trenches. Women fighting for their kingdom marriages. Women questioning their promise. But over and over, I found myself telling them: this isn't just about your man. This is about your *mandate*. This is about choosing *you*. Choosing healing. Choosing confidence. Choosing holiness. Choosing to return the promise to the One who gave it. Because if God joined it together, not even your own doubt can put it asunder.

God will finish what He started. And this book—this raw, weighty, unfiltered book—is evidence that He's doing just that.

Every page drips with obedience. Every chapter was a press. Every revelation was a release. And in that pressing, I found purpose. In that pouring, I found power. This isn't a guide to get a husband. This is a call to get in position. To become the woman who can carry what she's been praying for. To die to fantasy and rise in faith. To crucify the idol of ease and

---

45 *Esther 4:14 (NIV)* — *"And who knows but that you have come to your royal position for such a time as this?"*

step boldly into the discomfort of destiny. To stop asking for pretty prayers and start praying prophetic ones.

God chose me to be a mouthpiece. And I take that seriously. I'm not here to impress. I'm here to impact. I want every woman who reads this to glean wisdom. I want this to shake something loose in them. I want this to make them dig. To discover. To remember. To become. Because your purpose isn't on pause while you wait for the promise—your purpose *is* the preparation.

This book was birthed in just 14 days. Two weeks of yielded obedience and divine urgency. That alone is proof of supernatural acceleration—because when God is in it, He can do in days what should take years. This wasn't rushed; it was *released*. And that's what I gave Him—not perfection, just permission.

So, I leave nothing on the table. I renounce fear. I reject shame. I refuse to be silent. I don't want to live half-obedient. I don't want to die with potential still in my bones. I want to reach the full measure of what God intended. I want to hear "well done."

This is my legacy. Not what I leave behind, but what I *live* right now. I am Leah. Not the one they picked first. But the one God positioned. Misunderstood, mishandled, but never misaligned. Because when God puts His hand on you, no rejection can rewrite your role. *I am a Chosen Leah.*

And even if the promise still has mountains to climb… even if the story is still being written… even if the applause never comes—*I am still chosen.*

For Such a Time as This — Yielded for the Mantle

I did not choose the fire, but I chose to stay in it.
I did not seek the spotlight, but I didn't shrink from the mantle.
I said yes when silence felt safer—yes when shame
whispered *stay small.*
Yes when obedience cost me my comfort, but never my calling.

Legacy isn't loud. It's laced in quiet yeses, in oil-stained
journals, in tears wiped in secret while still choosing to
serve.
It's forged in surrender, not spotlight.
Born in the hidden, built to echo.

I am not the girl they expected.
I am the woman God appointed.
Not perfect, but postured.
Not elevated by man, but established by heaven.

I don't carry titles—I carry truth.
I carry testimony.
I carry time-tested obedience that hell couldn't stop and
fear couldn't silence.

This is not just a chapter. It's a charge.
A trumpet to every daughter still doubting:
*Your yes still matters. Your oil still speaks. Your voice still breaks
chains.*

And even if the promise looks unfinished—
You are still chosen.

Acknowledgments

To God be the glory. You saw me—*really* saw me—and still called me chosen. You shaped every word, every chapter, and every moment that led to this offering. I'm honored You trusted me with this story. Thank You for refining me, for carrying me, for awakening the mantle I didn't even know I had. I surrender it all back to You. This is Yours.

To my husband, Will—thank you for walking this journey with me. Our covenant has been both a mirror and a ministry. Thank you for covering me, challenging me, loving me, and growing with me. I honor the man you are and the man you're becoming. I pray this book serves as both a testimony and a reminder that *God finishes what He starts.*

To my spiritual leadership—Pastor Daniel and Pastor Cheryl Montgomery, and Pastor Jason and Pastor Carol Morris—thank you for believing in me, covering me, and stewarding the call of God on my life with such care. Your leadership is oil to me.

To my covenant sisters—Jessica, Kendie, and Prophetess (you know who you are)—thank you for standing in the gap, praying in the shadows, and reminding me of who I am when I nearly forgot. Our sisterhood is not casual, it's Kingdom.

To Kristal, who spoke destiny over me and pulled the call to the surface—I know you didn't do it for recognition, but I recognize heaven in you. Your obedience sparked mine.

To my Abundant Life family, thank you for being soil. Thank you for being a house where I could be planted, pruned, poured out, and still protected.

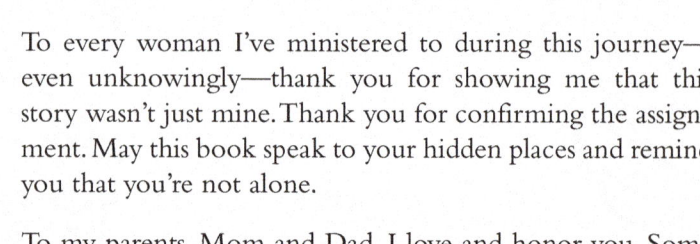

To every woman I've ministered to during this journey—even unknowingly—thank you for showing me that this story wasn't just mine. Thank you for confirming the assignment. May this book speak to your hidden places and remind you that you're not alone.

To my parents, Mom and Dad, I love and honor you. Some of these chapters were heavy, and I know parts of this story may be hard to hear. But I pray you can read it through the lens of healing, not blame. Thank you for your role in my becoming. I hope you're proud of the woman I am today.

And lastly, to myself—Leah, thank you for not quitting. Thank you for saying yes over and over again. Thank you for choosing surrender when fear tried to silence you. By the power of the Holy Spirit, you kept going. And look what God did.

Legacy in Motion

I don't know everything God intends to do with this book. I didn't plan to write it—He whispered, and I obeyed. This was never about building a platform; it was about saying *yes* to His call and faithfully stewarding the mantle He's entrusted to me, even when I can't see the full picture.

But if this story found you in the hidden place, if it met you in the middle of your wilderness, your promise, or your process, I'd love to hear from you. There's power in sharing testimony, in linking arms in transparency, and in trusting that healing can happen when we walk together in community.

You can find me online if you feel led—

Website: www.leahvadolkirk.com
Instagram: @the.chosen.leah
Facebook: Leah VaDol

I'm still listening. Still yielding. Still becoming.
And this—this book—is just the beginning

Prayer of Commission

Father,

I thank You for the one who made it to this final page—not by accident, but by divine appointment. You saw them. You called them. And through these pages, You've whispered to places in them that no one else could reach. I pray now that every seed planted in their heart would take root in good soil.

I declare that fear will not muzzle their voice. Shame will not hold their legacy hostage. Delay will not define their story. I speak freedom over every place they've questioned their worth, their assignment, their capacity to carry what You've placed inside them.

Lord, awaken every dormant dream. Stir up the gifts. Reignite the oil. Show them that their wilderness was not wasted—it was worship. Remind them that the promise is still alive, even if it looks buried. That *You* still finish what You start.

I pray boldness to obey, even when it costs. Clarity in the midst of confusion. Strength when surrender feels too heavy. May they walk with fresh fire, anchored identity, and unapologetic purpose. May they rise as the woman You always knew they were. The woman hidden for a season but revealed for such a time as this.

May their yes echo.
May their oil pour freely.
And may their legacy outlive them.

In Jesus' name,
Amen.

With love,
Leah VaDol Kirk